Studio

AQA GCSE French
Foundation
Vocabulary Book

Pearson

Published by Pearson Education Limited, 80 Strand, London, WC2R 0RL
www.pearsonschoolsandfecolleges.co.uk
Text © Pearson Education Limited 2017
Editorial management by Gwladys Rushworth for Haremi
Edited by Fabienne Tartarin
Typeset by York Publishing Solutions Pvt. Ltd.
Cover image: Alamy Images: kevers
Cover © Pearson Education Limited 2017

Written by Angela Stanley

First published 2017
10 9 8

British Library Cataloguing in Publication Data
A catalogue record for this book is available from the British Library.
ISBN 978 1 292 17256 9

Copyright notice
All rights reserved. No part of this publication may be reproduced in any form or by any means (including photocopying or storing it in any medium by electronic means and whether or not transiently or incidentally to some other use of this publication) without the written permission of the copyright owner, except in accordance with the provisions of the Copyright, Design and Patents Act 1988 or under the terms of a license issued by the Copyright Licensing Agency, Barnard's Inn, 86 Fetter Lane, London EC4A 1EN (www.cla.co.uk). Applications for the copyright owner's written permission should be addressed to the publisher.

Printed in the UK by Ashford Colour Press

Contenu

High-frequency words 4

Module 1
Words I should know for speaking and writing activities 15
Extra words I should know for reading and listening activities 18

Module 2
Words I should know for speaking and writing activities 19
Extra words I should know for reading and listening activities 22

Module 3
Words I should know for speaking and writing activities 23
Extra words I should know for reading and listening activities 26

Module 4
Words I should know for speaking and writing activities 27
Extra words I should know for reading and listening activities 30

Module 5
Words I should know for speaking and writing activities 31
Extra words I should know for reading and listening activities 34

Module 6
Words I should know for speaking and writing activities 35
Extra words I should know for reading and listening activities 38

Module 7
Words I should know for speaking and writing activities 40
Extra words I should know for reading and listening activities 43

Module 8
Words I should know for speaking and writing activities 44
Extra words I should know for reading and listening activities 47

High-frequency words

Common –er verbs

accepter	to accept
adorer	to love, to adore
aider	to help
aimer	to like
aller	to go
aller à pied	to walk
allumer	to light, to turn, to switch on
améliorer	to improve
(s)'arrêter	to stop

Had a look ☐ **Nearly there** ☐ **Nailed it** ☐

chanter	to sing
chercher	to look for
cliquer	to click (ICT)
coller	to stick
commander	to order
compter/compter sur	to count, to intend, to count on (someone)
contacter	to contact
continuer	to continue, to carry on
copier	to copy
se coucher	to go to bed
coûter	to cost

Had a look ☐ **Nearly there** ☐ **Nailed it** ☐

se débrouiller	to cope, to manage, to get by
décider	to decide
décoller	to take off (plane)
se dépêcher	to hurry
dépenser	to spend (money)
se déshabiller	to get undressed
désirer	to want, to desire
dessiner	to draw
détester	to hate
discuter	to discuss
donner	to give
durer	to last

Had a look ☐ **Nearly there** ☐ **Nailed it** ☐

s'échapper	to escape
écouter	to listen
écraser	to squash
empêcher	to prevent
endommager	to harm, to damage
entrer	to enter, to go in
envoyer	to send
espérer	to hope
essayer	to try
étudier	to study
expliquer	to explain

Had a look ☐ **Nearly there** ☐ **Nailed it** ☐

se fâcher	to get angry
fermer	to close, to switch off
frapper	to knock, to hit
gagner	to earn, to win
garder	to look after, to mind (child, dog)
garer	to park
gérer	to manage (business)
s'habiller	to get dressed
habiter	to live (inhabit)
informer	to inform
inviter	to invite
jeter	to throw

Had a look ☐ **Nearly there** ☐ **Nailed it** ☐

laisser	to leave behind (an object)
(se) laver	to wash
se lever	to get up
louer	to rent, to hire
manger	to eat
manquer	to miss, to be lacking
marcher	to walk, to work (function)
mériter	to deserve
monter	to climb, to get on(to), to go up
monter (dans)	to get into (bus, car, train)
montrer	to show
nettoyer	to clean
noter	to note

Had a look ☐ **Nearly there** ☐ **Nailed it** ☐

s'occuper de	to look after
organiser	to organise
ôter	to take off (clothes etc.)
oublier	to forget, to leave something behind
pardonner	to forgive
parler	to speak
passer	to pass, to spend (time)
penser	to think (about)

High-frequency words

peser	to weigh	tirer	to pull
pleurer	to cry	tomber	to fall
porter	to wear	toucher	to touch
poser	to place	travailler	to work
pousser	to push	traverser	to cross, to go across
préférer	to prefer	trouver	to find
présenter	to introduce (a person), to present		

Had a look ☐ **Nearly there** ☐ **Nailed it** ☐

prêter	to lend
se promener	to go for a walk
quitter	to leave (somewhere, somebody)

utiliser	to use
vérifier	to check
voler	to fly, to steal
voyager	to travel

Had a look ☐ **Nearly there** ☐ **Nailed it** ☐   **Had a look** ☐ **Nearly there** ☐ **Nailed it** ☐

raconter	to tell, to recount	**Common –ir verbs**	
se rappeler	to remember	atterrir	to land
rater	to fail, to miss (train, bus, etc.)	choisir	to choose
		s'endormir	to fall asleep
rechercher	to research	finir	to finish, to end
recommander	to recommend	nourrir	to feed, to nourish
regretter	to regret, to be sorry	offrir	to offer, to give a present/gift
rembourser	to refund		
remercier	to thank	ouvrir	to open
remplacer	to replace	partir	to leave, to depart
rencontrer	to meet	prévenir	to warn
rentrer (à la maison)	to return (home), to go back (home)	remplir	to fill, to fill in
		réussir	to succeed
renverser	to knock over	se servir de	to use
réparer	to repair	sortir	to go out
répéter	to repeat	se souvenir	to remember
se reposer	to rest	tenir	to hold
réserver	to reserve	venir	to come
ressembler	to look like, to resemble		

Had a look ☐ **Nearly there** ☐ **Nailed it** ☐

rester	to stay		
retourner (à l'école)	to return (to school), to go back (to school)	**Common –re verbs**	
		apprendre	to learn
se réveiller	to wake up	attendre	to wait for
rouler	to go (in a car)	boire	to drink

Had a look ☐ **Nearly there** ☐ **Nailed it** ☐

		conduire	to drive
		connaître	to know (person, place)
sauter	to jump	décrire	to describe
sauver	to save	descendre (de)	to get out of (bus, car, train)
sembler	to seem	dire	to tell, to say
signer	to sign	entendre	to hear
signifier	to mean, to signify	éteindre	to switch off
sonner	to ring (a bell)	(se) faire mal	to hurt (oneself)
souhaiter	to wish	introduire	to introduce (an item, an idea)
stationner	to park		
téléphoner	to phone	lire	to read
(se) terminer	to end		

Had a look ☐ **Nearly there** ☐ **Nailed it** ☐

High-frequency words

mettre	to put
plaire (à)	to please
prendre	to take
produire	to produce
remettre	to put back
répondre	to reply
rire	to laugh
sourire	to smile
suivre	to follow
vivre	to live
vendre	to sell

Had a look ☐ Nearly there ☐ Nailed it ☐

Common –oir verbs

avoir	to have
avoir besoin de	to need
avoir l'intention de (faire)	to mean to (do)
devoir	to have to, to must
savoir	to know (a fact)
voir	to see
vouloir	to want

Had a look ☐ Nearly there ☐ Nailed it ☐

Common adjectives: describing someone

actif/-ve	active
agréable	pleasant
amical(e)	friendly
bavard(e)	talkative
bête	silly
calme	peaceful, quiet, calm
désagréable	unpleasant
drôle	funny (comical)
égoïste	selfish
généreux/-euse	generous
gentil(le)	kind
gros(se)	fat
honnête	honest
indépendant(e)	independent
intelligent(e)	intelligent, clever
joli(e)	pretty
laid(e)	ugly
marrant(e)	funny (comical)
méchant(e)	naughty
mince	slim

Had a look ☐ Nearly there ☐ Nailed it ☐

moche	ugly
mûr(e)	mature
optimiste	optimistic
paresseux/-euse	lazy
(im)patient(e)	(im)patient
pessimiste	pessimistic
petit(e)	small, short (person)
(im)poli(e)	(im)polite
populaire	popular
responsable	responsible
rigolo(te)	funny (comical)
sage	good (well-behaved), wise
sérieux/-euse	serious
sévère	strict
strict(e)	strict
sympa (invariable)	nice, likeable
sympathique	nice, likeable
timide	shy
travailleur/-euse	hard-working
vilain(e)	naughty

Had a look ☐ Nearly there ☐ Nailed it ☐

Common adjectives: I am, you are, we are …

célèbre	famous
content(e)	pleased
de bonne humeur	in a good mood
étonné(e)	surprised
faible (en maths, etc.)	weak (in maths, etc.)
fatigué(e)	tired
fort(e) (en maths, etc.)	strong (in maths, etc.)
heureux/-euse	happy, content
inquiet/-iète	worried
jeune	young
malheureux/-euse	unhappy
perdu(e)	lost
pressé(e)	in a hurry
reconnaissant(e)	grateful
riche	rich
satisfait(e)	satisfied
sauf/-ve	safe
surpris(e)	surprised
triste	sad
vieux/vieil/vieille	old

Had a look ☐ Nearly there ☐ Nailed it ☐

Common adjectives: opinions

amusant(e)	fun, amusing
bruyant(e)	noisy
cher/-ère	expensive
chouette	great (fantastic)
démodé(e)	old fashioned
dur(e)	hard
effrayant(e)	frightening

High-frequency words

facile	*easy, simple*	haut	*high, tall (building)*
fantastique	*fantastic*	léger/-ère	*light*
fatigant(e)	*tiring*	libre	*free (unoccupied, available)*
favori(te)	*favourite*	long(ue)	*long*
formidable	*great (marvellous)*	lourd(e)	*heavy*
génial(e)	*great (fantastic)*		
idéal(e)	*ideal*		
incroyable	*unbelievable*		
injuste	*unfair*		
inutile	*useless*		
juste	*fair*		

Had a look ☐ **Nearly there** ☐ **Nailed it** ☐

		même	*same*
		moderne	*modern*
		mouillé(e)	*wet*
		mûr(e)	*ripe*
magnifique	*magnificent*	neuf/-ve	*new (brand new)*
malsain(e)	*unhealthy*	nombreux/-euse	*numerous*
merveilleux/-euse	*marvellous*	normal(e)	*normal*
nécessaire	*necessary*	nouveau/nouvel/nouvelle	*new*
négatif/-ve	*negative*	ouvert(e)	*open*

Had a look ☐ **Nearly there** ☐ **Nailed it** ☐

parfait(e)	*perfect*		
passionnant(e)	*exciting*	pareil(le)	*alike, the same*
positif/-ve	*positive*	plein(e)	*full*
pratique	*practical*	pourri(e)	*rotten*
préféré(e)	*favourite*	prêt(e)	*ready*
raisonnable	*reasonable*	prochain(e)	*next*
ridicule	*ridiculous*	propre	*own*
sain(e)	*healthy (food/way of life)*	rangé(e)	*tidy*
sensationnel(le)	*sensational*	rapide	*fast*
sensass	*sensational*	récent(e)	*recent*
super	*great (fantastic)*	reconnu(e)	*recognised, well known*
simple	*easy, simple*	réel(le)	*real*
superbe	*superb*	silencieux/-ieuse	*silent*
utile	*useful*	situé(e)	*situated*
valable	*valid*	tranquille	*peaceful, quiet, calm*
vrai(e)	*true*	type	*typical*

Had a look ☐ **Nearly there** ☐ **Nailed it** ☐

Other common adjectives

à la mode	*fashionable*
ancien(ne)	*former, old*
autre	*other*
chaud(e)	*hot*
court(e)	*short*
d'une grande valeur	*valuable*
dernier/-ière	*last*
étroit(e)	*thin, narrow*
fermé à clef	*locked*
grand(e)	*large, big*
gratuit(e)	*free (at no cost)*
grave	*serious*
gros(se)	*large, big*

Comparisons/Superlatives

plus/moins	*more/less*
plus que/moins que	*more than/less than*
bon/meilleur/le meilleur	*good/better/best*
mauvais/pire/le pire	*bad/worse/worst*
bien/mieux/le mieux	*well/better/best*
mal/plus mal/le plus mal	*badly/worse/worst*
beaucoup/plus/le plus	*a lot, lots/more/the most*
peu/moins/le moins	*few, little/less/the least*

Had a look ☐ **Nearly there** ☐ **Nailed it** ☐

Common adverbs

à peine	*hardly*
assez	*fairly, quite*

High-frequency words

aussi	too, as well	au fond	in the background, at the back
trop	too	au fond de	at the back of, at the bottom of
bien	well	au lieu de	instead of
bientôt	soon	au milieu (de)	in the middle (of)
bon marché	cheap(ly)	au premier plan	in the foreground
d'habitude	usually	au-dessus de	above
debout	standing	autour de	around
déjà	already	avant	before
encore	again	avec	with
ensemble	together	chez	at (someone's house)
fort	loud(ly)	contre	against
(mal)heureusement	(un)fortunately	dans	in (inside)
ici	here	de	from
immédiatement	immediately	dehors	outside
jamais	never		
là	there		
là-bas	over there		
là-haut	up there		
longtemps	(for) a long time		

Had a look ☐ **Nearly there** ☐ **Nailed it** ☐

		depuis	since, for
		derrière	behind
		devant	in front of, in the front
normalement	usually	en	in, within (time)
nulle part	nowhere	en dehors de	outside (of)
partout	everywhere	en face de	opposite
pas encore	not yet	en haut	above
peut-être	perhaps	en-dessous	under/underneath
plutôt	rather	entre	between
presque	almost	jusqu'à	until
quelque part	somewhere	loin de	far from
quelquefois	sometimes	malgré	despite, in spite of
rarement	rarely	nulle part	nowhere
récemment	recently	par	through
souvent	often	parmi	among(st)
surtout	especially	pour	for, in order to
toujours	always, still	près (de)	near (to)
tout de suite	straight away, immediately	sans	without
très	very	selon	according to
vite	quickly	sous	under/underneath
vraiment	really	sur	on (on top of)
		vers	towards

Had a look ☐ **Nearly there** ☐ **Nailed it** ☐

Had a look ☐ **Nearly there** ☐ **Nailed it** ☐

Prepositions

à	at, to
à côté de	next to
à partir de	from
à travers	across
après	after
au bord de	at the side/edge of
au bout de	at the end of

Connectives

à cause de	because of
à part	apart from
ainsi	so, therefore
alors	so, therefore, then
aussi	also
car	because
cependant	however

High-frequency words

c'est-à-dire	that is to say, i.e.	vingt-trois	23
comme	as, like	vingt-quatre	24
d'un côté/de l'autre côté	on the one hand/on the other hand	vingt-cinq	25
		vingt-six	26
donc	so, therefore	vingt-sept	27

Had a look ☐ **Nearly there** ☐ **Nailed it** ☐

		vingt-huit	28
		vingt-neuf	29
ensuite	next	trente	30
évidemment	obviously	trente et un	31
mais	but	trente-deux, etc.	32, etc.
même si	even if	quarante	40
ou	or	cinquante	50
par contre	on the other hand	soixante	60

Had a look ☐ **Nearly there** ☐ **Nailed it** ☐

par exemple	for example		
pendant que	while		
pourtant	however	soixante-dix	70
puis	then	soixante et onze	71
puisque	seeing that, since	soixante-douze	72
quand	when	soixante-treize	73
sans doute	undoubtedly, without doubt, probably	soixante-quatorze	74
		soixante-quinze	75
si	if	soixante-seize	76
y compris	including	soixante-dix-sept	77

Had a look ☐ **Nearly there** ☐ **Nailed it** ☐

soixante-dix-huit	78
soixante-dix-neuf	79

Numbers

Had a look ☐ **Nearly there** ☐ **Nailed it** ☐

un(e)	1		
deux	2		
trois	3	quatre-vingts	80
quatre	4	quatre-vingt-un	81
cinq	5	quatre-vingt-deux, etc.	82, etc.
six	6	quatre-vingt-dix	90
sept	7	quatre-vingt-onze	91
huit	8	quatre-vingt-douze, etc.	92, etc.

Had a look ☐ **Nearly there** ☐ **Nailed it** ☐

neuf	9		
dix	10		
onze	11	cent (m)	100
douze	12	cent un(e)	101
treize	13	cent vingt	120
quatorze	14	deux cents	200
quinze	15	mille (m)	1000
seize	16	mille cent	1100
dix-sept	17	deux mille	2000
dix-huit	18	un million (m)	1,000,000
dix-neuf	19	deux millions (m)	2,000,000
		premier/-ière	first

Had a look ☐ **Nearly there** ☐ **Nailed it** ☐

deuxième	second
vingt	20
vingt et un	21
vingt-deux	22

onzième	eleventh
vingt-et-unième	twenty first

Had a look ☐ **Nearly there** ☐ **Nailed it** ☐

High-frequency words

Opinions

à mon avis	in my opinion
absolument	absolutely
bien entendu	of course
bien sûr	of course
ça dépend	that depends
ça m'énerve	it gets on my nerves
ça me fait rire	it makes me laugh
ça me plaît	I like it
ça m'est égal	it's all the same to me
ça ne me dit rien	it means nothing to me, I don't fancy that, I don't feel like it
ça suffit	that's enough
ça ne fait rien	it doesn't matter
ce n'est pas la peine	it's not worth it
d'accord	OK (in agreement)
j'en ai assez/marre	I've had enough
personnellement	personally

Had a look ☐ **Nearly there** ☐ **Nailed it** ☐

Other useful expressions

à bientôt	see you soon
à demain/vendredi	see you tomorrow/on Friday
bonne chance	good luck
bon courage	good luck
Ça s'écrit comment?	How do you spell that?
ça va	I'm fine, it's OK
comme ci, comme ça	so-so
désolé(e)	sorry
défense de	you are not allowed to
dommage	what a shame
excuse-/excusez-moi	(I'm) sorry (informal/formal)
il est interdit de	you are not allowed to

Had a look ☐ **Nearly there** ☐ **Nailed it** ☐

il faut	you must/one must
il y a	there is/are
je ne comprends pas	I don't understand
je ne sais pas	I don't know
merci (bien)	thank you (very much)
Qu'est-ce que cela veut dire?	What does that mean?
avec plaisir	with pleasure
tant mieux	all/so much the better
tant pis	too bad
voici	here is/are
voilà	there is/are (i.e. over there)
volontiers	with pleasure

Had a look ☐ **Nearly there** ☐ **Nailed it** ☐

Other useful little words

ça/cela	that
le chiffre	figure (number)
la chose	thing
comme	as, like
la façon	way (manner)
la fois	time (occasion)
le genre	type (kind of)
madame	Mrs, Madam
mademoiselle	Miss
monsieur	Mr, Sir
le nombre	number
le numéro	number (phone number)
par exemple	for example
quelqu'un	someone
quelque chose	something
sauf	except
la sorte	type (kind of)
tout le monde	everybody

Had a look ☐ **Nearly there** ☐ **Nailed it** ☐

Time, frequency and sequencing expressions

à ... heure(s)	at ... o'clock
à ... heure(s) et quart	at quarter past ...
à ... heure(s) et demie	at half past ...
à ... heure(s) moins le quart	at quarter to ...
à la fois	at the same time
à l'avenir	in future, from now on
à l'heure	on time
à temps partiel	part-time
l'an (m)	year
l'année (f)	year
après	after
après-demain	the day after tomorrow
après-midi	afternoon
aujourd'hui	today
auparavant	formerly, in the past
avant	before
avant-hier	the day before yesterday
bientôt	soon

Had a look ☐ **Nearly there** ☐ **Nailed it** ☐

d'abord	at first, firstly
dans le futur	in the future
d'habitude	usually
de bonne heure	early
le début	start
demain	tomorrow

High-frequency words

dernier/dernière	last	tout à coup	suddenly, all of a sudden
de temps en temps	from time to time	tout de suite	immediately
déjà	already	vite	quickly
de nouveau	again		
en attendant	whilst waiting (for), meanwhile		

Had a look ☐ Nearly there ☐ Nailed it ☐

en avance	in advance
en ce moment	at the moment
en retard	late
en train de (faire…)	(to be) doing
en même temps	at the same time
encore une fois	once more, again
enfin	at last, finally
environ	about, approximately

Question words

Comment?	How?
Combien (de)?	How much, How many?
Que?	What?
Qu'est-ce qui?	What? (as subject)
Qu'est-ce que?	What? (as object)
Quoi?	What?
De quelle couleur?	What colour?
Comment?	What like?
À quelle heure?	(At) what time?
Quel/Quelle?	What/which?
Quand?	When?
Où?	Where?
Lequel/Laquelle/Lesquels/Lesquelles?	Which one(s)?
Qui?	Who?
Pourquoi?	Why?

Had a look ☐ Nearly there ☐ Nailed it ☐

la fin	end
hier	yesterday
il y a	ago
le jour	day
la journée	day
le lendemain	the next day
longtemps	for a long time
maintenant	now
le matin	morning
le mois	month
normalement	normally
la nuit	night
parfois	sometimes
le passé	past
pendant	during
plus tard	later
presque	almost, nearly
prochain	next

Had a look ☐ Nearly there ☐ Nailed it ☐

Colours

blanc(he)	white
bleu(e)	blue
brun(e)	brown
châtain (invariable)	chestnut brown
clair(e)	light
foncé(e)	dark
gris(e)	grey
jaune	yellow
marron (invariable)	brown, chestnut brown
noir(e)	black
rose	pink
rouge	red
vert(e)	green
violet(te)	violet

quelquefois	sometimes
rarement	rarely
récemment	recently
la semaine	week
seulement	only
le siècle	century
le soir	evening
soudain	suddenly
souvent	often
suivant	following
sur le point de (être)	(to be) about to
tard	late
tôt	early
toujours	always, still
tous les jours	every day

Had a look ☐ Nearly there ☐ Nailed it ☐

Days, months and seasons of the year

lundi	Monday
mardi	Tuesday
mercredi	Wednesday
jeudi	Thursday
vendredi	Friday
samedi	Saturday
dimanche	Sunday

Had a look ☐ Nearly there ☐ Nailed it ☐

High-frequency words

le mois	month
janvier	January
février	February
mars	March
avril	April
mai	May
juin	June
juillet	July
août	August
septembre	September
octobre	October
novembre	November
décembre	December

Had a look ☐ **Nearly there** ☐ **Nailed it** ☐

la saison	season
(en) automne (m)	(in) autumn
(au) printemps (m)	(in) spring
(en) été (m)	(in) summer
(en) hiver (m)	(in) winter

Had a look ☐ **Nearly there** ☐ **Nailed it** ☐

Quantities and measures

assez (de)	enough
beaucoup (de)	a lot (of), many
un centilitre	centilitre
un centimètre	centimetre
demi	half
une gramme	gramme
un kilomètre	kilometre
un mètre	metre
moins (de)	less
more encore (de)	(some)
pas mal (de)	quite a few
(un) peu (de)	a little of, few
plus (de)	more
plusieurs	several
le poids	weight
la quantité	quantity
un quart	quarter
quelques	some
un tiers	third
trop (de)	too much, too many

Had a look ☐ **Nearly there** ☐ **Nailed it** ☐

un kilo (de)	a kilo (of)
un litre (de)	a litre (of)
un morceau (de)	a piece (of)
un paquet (de)	a packet (of)
un peu (de)	a little (of)
un pot (de)	a jar (of)
une boîte (de)	a tin (of), a box (of)
une bouteille (de)	a bottle (of)
une centaine (de)	about a hundred
une douzaine (de)	a dozen
une tranche (de)	a slice (of)
une vingtaine (de)	about twenty

Had a look ☐ **Nearly there** ☐ **Nailed it** ☐

Countries

l'Algérie (f)	Algeria
l'Allemagne (f)	Germany
l'Angleterre (f)	England
l''Autriche (f)	Austria
la Belgique	Belgium
le Canada	Canada
la Chine	China
le Danemark	Denmark
la France	France
la Grande-Bretagne	Great Britain
la Grèce	Greece
la Hollande	Holland

Had a look ☐ **Nearly there** ☐ **Nailed it** ☐

l'Inde (f)	India
l'Irlande (f)	Ireland
l'Italie (f)	Italy
les Pays-Bas (m)	the Netherlands
le Pakistan	Pakistan
la Russie	Russia
l'Écosse (f)	Scotland
le Sénégal	Senegal
l'Espagne (f)	Spain
la Suisse	Switzerland
la Tunisie	Tunisia
la Turquie	Turkey
le Royaume-Uni	United Kingdom
les États-Unis (m)	the United States
le pays de Galles	Wales

Had a look ☐ **Nearly there** ☐ **Nailed it** ☐

Continents

l'Afrique (f)	Africa
l'Asie (f)	Asia
l'Australie (f)	Australia
l'Europe (f)	Europe
l'Amérique du Nord (f)	North America
l'Amérique du Sud (f)	South America

Had a look ☐ **Nearly there** ☐ **Nailed it** ☐

High-frequency words

Nationalities
algérien(ne)	*Algerian*
allemand(e)	*German*
américain(e)	*American*
anglais(e)	*English*
autrichien(ne)	*Austrian*
belge	*Belgian*
britannique	*British*
canadien(ne)	*Canadian*
chinois(e)	*Chinese*
corse	*Corsican*
danois(e)	*Danish*
écossais(e)	*Scottish*
espagnol(e)	*Spanish*
européen(ne)	*European*
français(e)	*French*
gallois(e)	*Welsh*
grec(que)	*Greek*
hollandais(e)	*Dutch*

Had a look ☐   **Nearly there** ☐   **Nailed it** ☐

indien(ne)	*Indian*
irlandais(e)	*Irish*
italien(ne)	*Italian*
pakistanais(e)	*Pakistani*
russe	*Russian*
suisse	*Swiss*
tunisien(ne)	*Tunisian*
turque	*Turkish*

Had a look ☐   **Nearly there** ☐   **Nailed it** ☐

Geographical surroundings
à droite	*on/to the right*
à gauche	*on/to the left*
chez	*at the house of*
de chaque côté	*from each side*
de l'autre côté	*from the other side*
en bas	*down(stairs)*
en haut	*up(stairs)*
ici	*here*
là	*there*
là-bas	*over there*

Had a look ☐   **Nearly there** ☐   **Nailed it** ☐

la banlieue	*suburb*
la campagne	*countryside*
le centre-ville	*town centre*
la ville	*town*

Had a look ☐   **Nearly there** ☐   **Nailed it** ☐

loin de	*far from*
nulle part	*nowhere*
par	*by*
partout	*everywhere*
quelque part	*somewhere*
situé(e)	*situated*
tout droit	*straight ahead*
tout près	*very near*
toutes directions	*all directions*

Had a look ☐   **Nearly there** ☐   **Nailed it** ☐

l'est (m)	*east*
l'ouest (m)	*west*
le nord	*north*
le sud	*south*

Had a look ☐   **Nearly there** ☐   **Nailed it** ☐

Materials
l'argent (m)	*silver*
le béton	*concrete*
le bois	*wood*
le cuir	*leather*
le fer	*iron*
la laine	*wool*
l'or (m)	*gold*
la soie	*silk*
le verre	*glass*

Had a look ☐   **Nearly there** ☐   **Nailed it** ☐

Climate
l'averse (f)	*shower*
briller	*to shine*
le brouillard	*fog*
la brume	*mist*
la chaleur	*heat*
le ciel	*sky*
le climat	*climate*
couvert	*overcast*
doux	*mild*
l'éclair (m)	*lightning*
l'éclaircie (f)	*bright spell*
ensoleillé	*sunny*
faire beau	*to be fine (weather)*
faire mauvais	*to be bad (weather)*
geler	*to freeze*
la glace	*ice*
humide	*humid, wet*
la météo	*weather forecast*
mouillé	*wet*

Had a look ☐   **Nearly there** ☐   **Nailed it** ☐

High-frequency words

neiger	*to snow*
le nuage	*cloud*
nuageux	*cloudy*
l'ombre (f)	*shade, shadow*
l'orage (m)	*storm*
orageux	*stormy*
pleuvoir	*to rain*
la pluie	*rain*
sec	*dry*
la tempête	*storm*
le temps	*weather*
le tonnerre	*thunder*
tremper	*to soak*
le vent	*wind*

Had a look ☐ **Nearly there** ☐ **Nailed it** ☐

Social conventions

à plus tard	*see you later*
à tout à l'heure	*see you later*
allô	*hello (on the telephone)*
amitiés	*best wishes*
amuse-toi/amusez-vous bien!	*enjoy yourself/yourselves!*
au revoir	*goodbye*
au secours	*help!*
bien sûr	*of course*
bon voyage	*have a good journey*
bonjour	*hello, good morning*
bonne journée	*have a good day*
bonne nuit	*goodnight*
bonne soirée	*have a good evening*
bonsoir	*good evening*
de rien	*don't mention it*
Je t'/vous en prie	*It's a pleasure*
non merci	*no thank you*
pardon?	*I beg your pardon? Pardon?*
prière de	*please (request – formal)*
rendez-vous (m)	*meeting, meeting place*
rendez-vous à six heures	*meet you at 6 o'clock*
s'il te plaît/s'il vous plaît	*please (informal)/please (polite)*
salut	*hi*
veuillez	*please (request – formal)*

Had a look ☐ **Nearly there** ☐ **Nailed it** ☐

Module 1 Vocabulaire

Words I should know for speaking and writing activities

La famille / *Family members*

les parents (m)	*parents*
le père	*father*
la mère	*mother*
le beau-père	*stepfather, father-in-law*
la belle-mère	*stepmother, mother-in-law*
le mari	*husband*
la femme	*wife*
les enfants (m)	*children*
le fils	*son*
la fille	*daughter*
le frère	*brother*
la sœur	*sister*

Had a look ☐   Nearly there ☐   Nailed it ☐

le demi-frère	*half-brother, stepbrother*
la demi-sœur	*half-sister, stepsister*
le beau-frère	*brother-in-law*
la belle-sœur	*sister-in-law*
les grands-parents (m)	*grandparents*
le grand-père	*grandfather*
la grand-mère	*grandmother*
les petits-enfants (m)	*grandchildren*
le petit-fils	*grandson*
la petite-fille	*granddaughter*
l'oncle (m)	*uncle*
la tante	*aunt*
le cousin/la cousine	*cousin*

Had a look ☐   Nearly there ☐   Nailed it ☐

Les adjectifs de personnalité / *Personality adjectives*

Il/Elle est …	*He/She is …*
agaçant(e)	*annoying*
arrogant(e)	*arrogant*
amusant(e)	*amusing, funny*
bavard(e)	*talkative, chatty*
charmant(e)	*charming*
content(e)	*happy*
fort(e)	*strong*
impatient(e)	*impatient*
impoli(e)	*impolite*
indépendant(e)	*independent*
intelligent(e)	*intelligent*
marrant(e)	*funny*
méchant(e)	*nasty, mean*
têtu(e)	*stubborn, pig-headed*

Had a look ☐   Nearly there ☐   Nailed it ☐

Ma description physique / *My physical description*

J'ai les cheveux …	*I have …*
courts/longs	*short/long hair*
raides/bouclés/frisés	*straight/curly hair*
noirs/bruns/blonds	*black/brown/blond hair*
roux/gris/blancs	*red/grey/white hair*
J'ai les yeux …	*I have …*
bleus/verts	*blue/green eyes*
gris/marron	*grey/brown eyes*
J'ai …	*I have …*
des lunettes	*glasses*
des boutons	*spots*
une moustache	*a moustache*
une barbe	*a beard*
Je suis …	*I am …*
petit(e)/grand(e)	*short/tall*
de taille moyenne	*of average height*
mince/gros(se)	*thin/fat*

Had a look ☐   Nearly there ☐   Nailed it ☐

En ville / *In town*

la boîte de nuit	*night club*
le bowling	*bowling alley*
le café	*café*
le centre commercial	*shopping centre*
le cinéma	*cinema*
les magasins (m)	*shops*
la patinoire	*ice rink*
la piscine	*swimming pool*
la plage	*beach*
le théâtre	*theatre*
dans	*in*
derrière	*behind*
devant	*in front of*
entre	*between*

Had a look ☐   Nearly there ☐   Nailed it ☐

Quand? / *When?*

aujourd'hui	*today*
demain	*tomorrow*
ce/demain matin	*this/tomorrow morning*
cet/demain après-midi	*this/tomorrow afternoon*
ce/demain soir	*this/tomorrow evening*
lundi matin	*on Monday morning*
samedi soir	*on Saturday night*

Had a look ☐   Nearly there ☐   Nailed it ☐

Les amis / *Friends*

l'ami (m)/le copain	*(male) friend*
l'amie (f)/la copine	*(female) friend*
le petit ami/le petit copain	*boyfriend*

Module 1 Vocabulaire

la petite amie/la petite copine	*girlfriend*	**Les rapports de famille**	***Family relationships***
Je retrouve mes amis au parc.	*I meet up with my friends in the park.*	Je m'entends bien avec …	*I get on well with …*
Je traîne en ville avec mes copines.	*I hang out in town with my (female) friends.*	Je me dispute avec …	*I argue with …*
		Je me chamaille avec …	*I bicker with …*
Je tchatte en ligne avec ma meilleure copine.	*I chat online with my best (female) friend.*	Je m'amuse avec …	*I have fun with …*
		Je m'occupe de …	*I look after …*
Avec mon petit ami, j'écoute de la musique.	*I listen to music with my boyfriend.*	le frère aîné/cadet	*older/younger brother*
		la sœur aînée/cadette	*older/younger sister*
Je passe chez ma petite copine.	*I go to my girlfriend's house.*	Il/Elle est/a l'air/ semble …	*He/She is/looks/ seems …*
On rigole bien ensemble.	*We have a good laugh together.*	dynamique	*lively*
		égoïste	*selfish*
On regarde un film ou des clips vidéo.	*We watch a film or music videos.*	jaloux/-ouse	*jealous*
		sévère	*strict*
On joue au foot ou au basket ensemble.	*We play football or basketball together.*	timide	*shy*
		travailleur/-euse	*hard-working*
On discute de tout.	*We talk about everything.*		
On mange ensemble au fast-food.	*We eat together at a fast-food restaurant.*		

Had a look ☐ Nearly there ☐ Nailed it ☐

On va sortir	***Going out***		
Je vais …	*I am going …*		
aller à un match	*to go to a match*		
aller au bowling	*to go to the bowling alley*		
aller au cinéma	*to go to the cinema*		
aller à la piscine	*to go to the swimming pool*		
voir un spectacle	*to see a show*		
faire du patin à glace	*to go ice-skating*		
faire du skate	*to go skateboarding*		
faire les magasins	*to go shopping*		
jouer à des jeux vidéo	*to play video games*		
Tu veux venir?	*Do you want to come?*		

L'amitié	***Friendship***
Je pense que …	*I think that …*
Pour moi, …	*For me …*
À mon avis, …	*In my opinion …*
Un(e) bon(ne) ami(e) est …	*A good friend is …*
compréhensif/-ive	*understanding*
cool	*cool*
drôle	*funny*
fidèle	*loyal*
généreux/-euse	*generous*
gentil(le)	*kind*
honnête	*honest*
modeste	*modest*
optimiste	*optimistic*
patient(e)	*patient*
sensible	*sensitive*
sympa	*nice*

Had a look ☐ Nearly there ☐ Nailed it ☐

Les questions	***Questions***
Quand?	*When?*
Avec qui?	*With who/whom?*
On y va comment?	*How are we getting there?*
On se retrouve où?	*Where shall we meet?*
On se retrouve à quelle heure?	*At what time shall we meet?*

Had a look ☐ Nearly there ☐ Nailed it ☐

Un(e) bon(ne) ami(e) …	*A good friend …*
écoute mes problèmes/ mes secrets	*listens to my problems/ my secrets*
discute de tout avec moi	*talks about everything with me*
aide tout le monde	*helps everyone*
accepte mes imperfections	*accepts my faults*
respecte mes opinions	*respects my opinions*
a les mêmes centres d'intérêt que moi	*has the same interests as me*
a le sens de l'humour	*has a sense of humour*

Une sortie	***An outing***
J'ai contacté un copain/ une copine.	*I contacted a friend.*
J'ai quitté la maison.	*I left the house.*
J'ai raté le bus.	*I missed the bus.*
Je suis allé(e) en ville.	*I went into town.*
J'ai écouté de la musique.	*I listened to music.*
J'ai retrouvé mon copain/ma copine.	*I met up with my friend.*

Had a look ☐ Nearly there ☐ Nailed it ☐

Module 1 Vocabulaire

J'ai discuté avec mon copain/ma copine.	I talked to my friend.
J'ai mangé un sandwich.	I ate a sandwich.
J'ai acheté des vêtements.	I bought some clothes.
C'était super.	It was great.
J'ai passé une très bonne journée.	I had a very good day.

Had a look ☐ **Nearly there** ☐ **Nailed it** ☐

La personne que j'admire — The person I admire

Comment s'appelle la personne que tu admires?	What is the name of the person you admire?
Mon héros s'appelle …	My hero is called …
Mon héroïne s'appelle …	My heroine is called …
Mon modèle s'appelle …	My role model is called …
C'est qui?	Who is he/she?
C'est un pilote de Formule 1.	He is a Formula 1 driver.
C'est un scientifique.	He is a scientist.
C'est une actrice.	She is an actress.
C'est une créatrice de mode.	She is a fashion designer.
Fais-moi sa description physique.	Describe for me what he/she looks like.

Had a look ☐ **Nearly there** ☐ **Nailed it** ☐

Il/Elle est …	He/She is …
petit(e)/gros(se), etc.	small/fat, etc.
Il/Elle a les cheveux bruns, etc.	He/She has brown hair, etc.
Quelle est sa personnalité?	What is his/her personality?
Il/Elle est …	He/She is …
travailleur/-euse/ créatif/-ive, etc.	hard-working/creative, etc.
Pourquoi est-ce que tu admires cette personne?	Why do you admire this person?
J'admire (Stromae/Malala, etc.) car il/elle …	I admire (Stromae/Malala, etc.) because he/she …
a travaillé très dur	worked/has worked very hard
a joué dans beaucoup de films	acted/has acted in lots of films
a gagné beaucoup de courses	won/has won lots of races
a donné de l'argent à de bonnes œuvres	gave/has given money to good causes
a lutté contre ses problèmes	fought/has fought his/her problems
J'aimerais être comme lui/elle.	I would like to be like him/her.

Had a look ☐ **Nearly there** ☐ **Nailed it** ☐

17

Module 1 Vocabulaire

Extra words I should know for reading and listening activities

Moi — **Me**
Je suis … — I am …
Je m'appelle …* — I am called …
Je joue le rôle de … — I play the part of …

Had a look ☐ **Nearly there** ☐ **Nailed it** ☐

La personne que j'admire — **The person that I admire**
Il/elle a sauvé …** — he/she saved …
Il/elle a aidé …** — he/she helped …
ses vêtements — his/her clothes
ses romans — his/her novels
ses études — his/her studies
son exécution — his/her execution
sa créativité — his/her creativity
sa détermination — his/her determination
un enfant adopté — an adopted child
un(e) auteur(e) — an author

Had a look ☐ **Nearly there** ☐ **Nailed it** ☐

un(e) professeur(e) — a teacher
un exemple — an example
un soldat — a soldier
un(e) aviateur/-trice — an aviator
une armée — an army
un camp — a camp
une vie — a life
une université — a university
une maison — a house
une mode — a fashion

Had a look ☐ **Nearly there** ☐ **Nailed it** ☐

Comment est ton héros/héroïne? — **What is your hero/heroine like?**
Il/elle est/était … — He/she is/was …
courageux/-euse — brave
de nationalité (pakistanaise) — of (Pakistani) nationality
jeune — young
fort(e) — strong
francophone — French-speaking
mort(e) — dead
vrai(e) — real
algérien(ne) — Algerian

Had a look ☐ **Nearly there** ☐ **Nailed it** ☐

Une visite chez … — **A visit to …'s house**
On est invité(e)s à (manger) … — We were invited to (eat) …
On a pris le train tôt/tard. — We got the train early/late.
le matin — in the morning
le soir — in the evening

Had a look ☐ **Nearly there** ☐ **Nailed it** ☐

⭐ *Some verbs in French have three parts to them. Without the third part known as the reflexive pronoun, the verb changes its meaning, for example:

Je m'appelle …   I am called …

J'appelle le chien.   I call the dog.

Elle se lève.   She gets up.

Elle lève la chaise.   She lifts up the chair.

⭐ **Past tense actions often end in -é, for example: *Il/elle a aidé* (he/she helped). Without the é, the meaning of the word changes and its sound changes too.

When you read a word with é, or hear this sound, work out the context to find the meaning.

Module 2 Vocabulaire

Words I should know for speaking and writing activities

Les passe-temps	**Hobbies**
Je joue ...	I play ...
au badminton	badminton
au basket	basketball
au billard	snooker
au foot	football
au golf	golf
au hockey	hockey
au rugby	rugby
au tennis	tennis
au volley	volleyball
à la pétanque	French bowls
aux cartes (f)	cards
aux échecs (m)	chess
du piano	the piano
du saxophone	the saxophone
du violon	the violin
de la batterie	the drums
de la guitare	the guitar
de l'accordéon (m)	the accordion
de l'harmonica (m)	the harmonica

Had a look ☐   Nearly there ☐   Nailed it ☐

Les expressions de fréquence	**Frequency expressions**
tous les jours	every day
tous les soirs	every evening
tous les samedis	every Saturday
une fois par semaine	once a week
deux fois par semaine	twice a week
souvent	often
de temps en temps	from time to time
rarement	rarely

Had a look ☐   Nearly there ☐   Nailed it ☐

Les opinions	**Opinions**
Je trouve ça ...	I find that ...
cool/génial	cool/great
passionnant/super	exciting/super
ennuyeux/nul	boring/rubbish
stupide	stupid

Had a look ☐   Nearly there ☐   Nailed it ☐

J'aime et je n'aime pas ...	**I like and I don't like ...**
Ma passion, c'est ...	My passion is ...
le cinéma/le sport/la musique	the cinema/sport/music
J'aime/J'adore/Je préfère ...	I like/love/prefer ...
Je n'aime pas/Je déteste ...	I don't like/hate ...

le foot/jouer au foot	football/playing football
la lecture/lire	reading
la photographie/prendre des photos	photography/taking photos

Had a look ☐   Nearly there ☐   Nailed it ☐

Les films	**Films**
une comédie	a comedy
un western	a Western
un film fantastique	a fantasy film
un film d'action	an action film
un film d'arts martiaux	a martial arts film
un film d'aventure	an adventure film
un film d'horreur	a horror film
un film de gangsters	a gangster film
un film de science-fiction	a science fiction film

Had a look ☐   Nearly there ☐   Nailed it ☐

Acheter des billets	**Buying tickets**
Qu'est-ce qu'il y a au cinéma?	What's on at the cinema?
La séance commence à quelle heure?	At what time does the screening start?
Je peux vous aider?	Can I help you?
Je voudrais deux billets pour ...	I would like two tickets for ...
Pour quelle séance?	For which screening?
Pour la séance de 19 heures.	For the screening at 7 p.m.
Ça coûte combien?	How much does it cost?
Le tarif réduit, c'est 14 euros la place.	The reduced price is 14 euros per seat.

Had a look ☐   Nearly there ☐   Nailed it ☐

Le sport	**Sport**
Je fais ...	I ...
du footing	go jogging
du trampoline	do trampolining
du vélo	go cycling
de la boxe	do boxing
de la danse	go dancing
de la natation	go swimming
de l'équitation (f)	go horse-riding
de l'escalade (f)	go climbing
de l'escrime (f)	do fencing
des randonnées (f)	go hiking
Je fais ça depuis ...	I have been doing that for ...
six mois	six months
deux ans	two years

Had a look ☐   Nearly there ☐   Nailed it ☐

Module 2 Vocabulaire

Parler de sport
Je préfère les sports individuels.
Je préfère les sports d'équipe.
Je trouve ça rigolo/ facile/rapide
Ça me fait du bien.
Ça me détend.
Ça booste le moral.
C'est bon pour le corps et le mental.
Quand je fais ça, je respire
j'oublie mes soucis

Talking about sport
I prefer individual sports.
I prefer team sports.
I find it/that fun/easy/ fast
It does me good.
It relaxes me.
It boosts my/your mood.
It's good for the body and the mind.
When I do/I'm doing it, ...
I breathe
I forget my worries

Had a look ☐ Nearly there ☐ Nailed it ☐

Sur mon téléphone portable/ma tablette, ...
je crée des playlists
je télécharge de la musique
je regarde des clips vidéo
je joue à des jeux
je fais des recherches pour mes devoirs
je fais des achats
j'écris des messages
j'écris des articles pour mon blog
je lis mes e-mails
je vais sur des réseaux sociaux
je prends des photos
je mets mes photos sur Instagram ou Snapchat
À mon avis, c'est ...
génial
très pratique
indispensable

On my phone/tablet, ...
I create playlists
I download music
I watch music videos
I play games
I do research for my homework
I buy things
I write messages
I write posts for my blog
I read my emails
I go onto social media sites
I take photos
I put my photos on Instagram or Snapchat
In my opinion, it's ...
great
very practical
essential

Had a look ☐ Nearly there ☐ Nailed it ☐

Internet
Il est facile de/d' ...
Il est possible de/d' ...
rester en contact avec ses amis
faire des recherches pour ses devoirs
utiliser un dico en ligne
partager des photos
Il est dangereux de ...
partager ses détails personnels

The internet
It is easy to ...
It is possible to ...
stay in contact with your friends
do research for your homework
use an online dictionary
share photos
It is dangerous to ...
share your personal details

passer trop de temps sur Internet
tchatter en ligne avec des inconnus
Il est important de ... faire du sport
passer du temps avec sa famille
retrouver ses amis en vrai

spend too much time on the internet
chat to strangers online
It is important to ... do some sport
spend some time with your family
meet up with your friends in real life

Had a look ☐ Nearly there ☐ Nailed it ☐

La lecture
J'apprécie beaucoup les ...
Je préfère les ...
J'adore les ...
J'ai une passion pour les ...
Je n'aime pas les ...
J'ai horreur des ...
romans fantastiques
romans policiers
romans d'amour
livres d'épouvante
BD

mangas
J'aime les illustrations/ l'humour.
Je ne lis pas sur une tablette.
Je préfère tenir un livre traditionnel dans mes mains.
Je ne lis plus de livres traditionnels.
Je lis beaucoup en ligne.

Reading
I really appreciate/like ...
I prefer ...
I love ...
I'm passionate about ...
I don't like ...
I hate ...
fantasy novels
detective novels
romance novels
horror books
comic books, graphic novels
mangas
I like the illustrations/ humour.
I don't read on a tablet.
I prefer holding a traditional book in my hands.
I no longer read traditional books.
I read a lot online.

Had a look ☐ Nearly there ☐ Nailed it ☐

La musique
J'aime ... /Je n'aime pas ...
le jazz
le rap
le reggae
le rock
la musique classique
la musique pop
J'écoute ma musique ...
sur mon téléphone portable avec mes écouteurs.
sur mon ordi
sur une tablette
Je regarde des clips vidéo pour écouter ma musique.

Music
I like ... /I don't like ...
jazz
rap
reggae
rock
classical music
pop music
I listen to my music ...
on my phone with my earphones.
on my computer
on a tablet
I watch music videos to listen to my music.

Module 2 Vocabulaire

Mon chanteur préféré/ ma chanteuse préférée, c'est ... car ...	My favourite singer is ... because ...
j'aime ses paroles	I like his/her lyrics
j'aime ses mélodies	I like his/her tunes
sa musique me donne envie de danser	his/her music makes me want to dance
sa musique me donne envie de chanter	his/her music makes me want to sing

Had a look ☐ Nearly there ☐ Nailed it ☐

Les émissions de télé — *TV programmes*

J'aime/Je n'aime pas ...	I like/I don't like ...
les documentaires (m)	documentaries
les jeux télévisés (m)	game shows
les magazines culturels (m)	magazine programmes
les séries (f)	series
les émissions de sport (f)	sports programmes
les émissions de musique (f)	music programmes
les émissions de télé-réalité (f)	reality TV programmes
les actualités (f)	the news
parce qu'ils/elles sont ...	because they are/it is ...
amusant(e)s	funny
divertissant(e)s	entertaining
intéressant(e)s	interesting
passionnant(e)s	exciting
éducatifs/-ives	educational
ennuyeux/-euses	boring
(trop) sérieux/-euses	(too) serious
originaux/-ales	original

Had a look ☐ Nearly there ☐ Nailed it ☐

Mon émission préférée s'appelle ...	My favourite programme is called ...
C'est un jeu télévisé.	It's a game show.
C'est une série.	It's a drama series.
J'aime bien l'animateur/-rice.	I like the presenter.
Les acteurs sont très doués.	The actors are very talented.
Le scénario est passionnant.	The plot is exciting.
J'apprends beaucoup.	I learn a lot.
Je ne rate jamais cette émission!	I never miss this programme!

Had a look ☐ Nearly there ☐ Nailed it ☐

Une soirée entre amis — *An evening with friends*

Je suis allé(e) au cinéma.	I went to the cinema.
Je suis sorti(e) avec ...	I went out with ...
On est allé(e)s à un concert.	We went to a concert.
On a vu un film.	We saw a film.
On est allé(e)s en ville.	We went into town.
On a fait du patin à glace.	We went ice skating.
J'ai pris beaucoup de photos.	I took lots of photos.
J'ai mis les photos sur Instagram.	I put the photos on Instagram.
On est allé(e)s au restaurant.	We went to a restaurant.
J'ai bu un coca.	I drank a cola.
C'était ...	It was ...
génial	great
lamentable	pathetic
amusant	fun, funny
délicieux	delicious

Had a look ☐ Nearly there ☐ Nailed it ☐

Module 2 Vocabulaire

Extra words I should know for reading and listening activities

Tu es sportif/ sportive?	**Are you sporty?**
le marathon de (Paris)	the (Paris) marathon
les sports rapides (m)	quick sports
mon équipe (f)	my team
ensemble	together

Had a look ☐ Nearly there ☐ Nailed it ☐

Ma vie d'internaute	**My online life**
le blog*	blog
le dico** en ligne	online dictionary
le portable	laptop
la tablette*	tablet
l'ordi** (m)	computer
les réseaux sociaux (m)	social networks
les écouteurs (m)	headphones
apprendre beaucoup de choses	to learn a lot of things
partager des détails personnels avec des inconnus	to share your personal details with strangers
faire des achats	to do shopping
jouer à des jeux	to play games
la photographie	photography

Had a look ☐ Nearly there ☐ Nailed it ☐

Je (ne) lis (pas) …	I (don't) read …
Je trouve …	I find …
Je préfère …	I prefer …
Je pense …	I think …
Je regarde …	I watch …
Je peux …	I can …
J'adore …	I love …
J'aime (bien) …	I (really) like …
J'apprécie …	I appreciate …
J'écoute …	I listen …

Had a look ☐ Nearly there ☐ Nailed it ☐

*Lots of new technology-related words are the same in French as in English, for example: *le blog, la tablette*.

**Remember that you can abbreviate words in French too, for example: *ordi* (*ordinateur*), *dico* (*dictionnaire*). So, if you encounter a word that you don't recognise, think about whether it is a shorter version of a word that you already know. The context that the word is in will help you to do this.

Words I should know for speaking and writing activities

La nourriture et les boissons / *Food and drink*
du beurre / *butter*
du fromage / *cheese*
du lait / *milk*
du pain / *bread*
du poisson / *fish*
du poulet / *chicken*
du yaourt / *yoghurt*
de la confiture / *jam*
de la glace / *ice cream*
de la viande / *meat*
de l'eau (f) / *water*
des bananes (f) / *bananas*
des fraises (f) / *strawberries*
des œufs (m) / *eggs*
des pêches (f) / *peaches*
des poires (f) / *pears*
des pommes (f) / *apples*
des pommes de terre (f) / *potatoes*

Had a look ☐ Nearly there ☐ Nailed it ☐

Les repas / *Meals*
Qu'est-ce que tu prends pour le petit-déjeuner? / *What do you have for breakfast?*
Qu'est-ce que tu manges à midi? / *What do you eat at lunchtime?*
Qu'est-ce que tu manges comme casse-croûte? / *What do you have as a snack?*
Qu'est-ce que tu manges, le soir? / *What do you eat in the evening?*
Qu'est-ce que tu bois? / *What do you drink?*
Pour le petit-déjeuner, … / *For breakfast, …*
À midi, … / *At lunchtime, …*
Comme casse-croûte, … / *As a snack, …*
Le soir, … / *In the evening, …*
Comme dessert, … / *For dessert, …*
Je prends/Je mange … / *I have/I eat …*
des céréales (f) / *cereal*
du pain grillé / *toast*
un sandwich / *a sandwich*
des chips (f) / *crisps*
des biscuits (m) / *biscuits*
des pâtes (f) / *pasta*
de la salade / *salad*
de la glace au chocolat / *chocolate ice cream*
Je bois du jus d'orange. / *I drink orange juice.*

Had a look ☐ Nearly there ☐ Nailed it ☐

Les quantités / *Quantities*
un kilo de … / *a kilo of …*
deux cent cinquante grammes de … / *250 grams of …*
un litre de … / *a litre of …*
un paquet de … / *a packet of …*
un pot de … / *a jar/pot of …*
une boîte de … / *a tin/can of …*
une bouteille de … / *a bottle of …*
quatre tranches de … / *four slices of …*

Had a look ☐ Nearly there ☐ Nailed it ☐

Les vêtements / *Clothes*
Je porte … / *I wear/am wearing …*
un blouson / *a jacket*
un chapeau / *a hat*
un costume / *a suit*
un imperméable / *a raincoat*
un jean (moulant) / *(a pair of) (skinny) jeans*
un manteau / *a coat*
un pantalon / *(a pair of) trousers*
un polo / *a polo shirt*
un pull / *a jumper*
un sac à main / *a handbag*
un short / *(a pair of) shorts*
un sweat à capuche / *a hoody*
un tee-shirt / *a T-shirt*
une casquette / *a cap*
une ceinture / *a belt*

Had a look ☐ Nearly there ☐ Nailed it ☐

une chemise / *a shirt*
une écharpe / *a scarf*
une mini-jupe / *a miniskirt*
une montre / *a watch*
une robe / *a dress*
une veste / *a jacket*
des baskets (de marque) (f) / *(designer) trainers*
des boucles d'oreille (f) / *earrings*
des bottes (f) / *boots*
des chaussettes (f) / *socks*
des chaussures (f) / *shoes*
des gants (m) / *gloves*
des lunettes de soleil (f) / *sunglasses*
en laine / *woollen*
en cuir / *leather*
rayé(e)(s) / *striped*

Had a look ☐ Nearly there ☐ Nailed it ☐

Les couleurs / *Colours*
blanc(he)(s) / *white*
bleu(e)(s) / *blue*
gris(e)(s) / *grey*
jaune(s) / *yellow*
marron / *brown*

23

Module 3 Vocabulaire

mauve(s)	purple
noir(e)(s)	black
orange	orange
rose(s)	pink
rouge(s)	red
vert(e)(s)	green
clair	light
foncé	dark
multicolore(s)	multi-coloured

Had a look ☐   Nearly there ☐   Nailed it ☐

La vie quotidienne — *Daily life*

J'ai cours tous les jours sauf …	I have lessons every day except …
Les jours d'école, …	On school days …
je dois me lever tôt	I have to get up early
je dois quitter la maison à (7h30)	I have to leave the house at (7:30 a.m.)
Le soir, …	In the evening, …
je dois faire mes devoirs	I have to do my homework
je dois aider ma mère	I have to help my mother
je peux regarder un peu la télé	I can watch a bit of TV
Le samedi, …	On Saturdays, …
Le dimanche, …	On Sundays, …
je peux rester au lit	I can stay in bed
je peux retrouver mes copains/copines en ville	I can meet up with my friends in town
je dois ranger ma chambre	I have to tidy my room
je peux écouter de la musique	I can listen to music

Had a look ☐   Nearly there ☐   Nailed it ☐

Au magasin de vêtements — *In the clothes shop*

la taille	size
la pointure	shoe size
les cabines d'essayage (f)	changing rooms
une taille moyenne	medium size
Il y a un trou.	There's a hole (in it).
Il y a une tache.	There's a stain (on it).
Il/Elle est … /Ils/Elles sont …	It is … /They are …
trop petit(e)(s)	too small
trop grand(e)(s)	too big
cassé(e)(s)	broken
Il/Elle ne marche pas.	It is not working/ doesn't work.
Je voudrais …	I would like …
échanger (la jupe/le pantalon, etc.)	to exchange (the skirt/ trousers, etc.)
un remboursement	a refund

Had a look ☐   Nearly there ☐   Nailed it ☐

Faire les magasins ou faire du shopping en ligne? — *Go to the shops or shop online?*

Je préfère …	I prefer …
faire les magasins	to go to the shops
faire mes achats en ligne	to make my purchases online
parce que/qu' …	because …
c'est mieux d'essayer les vêtements dans un magasin	it's better to try clothes on in a shop
je peux demander l'opinion de mes ami(e)s	I can ask my friends' opinion
il y a trop de monde dans les magasins	there are too many people in the shops
on peut trouver des vêtements moins chers	you can find cheaper clothes
c'est plus facile/plus rapide	it's easier/faster

Had a look ☐   Nearly there ☐   Nailed it ☐

Les fêtes — *Festivals*

Noël	Christmas
la veille de Noël	Christmas Eve
Pâques	Easter
Divali	Diwali
Hanoukka	Hanukkah
Aïd-el-Fitr	Eid al-Fitr
le 6 janvier/la fête des Rois	Epiphany
le premier avril	April Fool's Day
la Chandeleur	Candlemas
le Nouvel An	New Year
la Saint-Sylvestre	New Year's Eve
la Saint-Valentin	Valentine's Day
la fête des Mères	Mother's Day
le 14 juillet/la fête nationale française	Bastille Day, 14 July
On est chrétiens.	We are Christian.
On est juifs.	We are Jewish.
On est musulmans.	We are Muslim.

Had a look ☐   Nearly there ☐   Nailed it ☐

Chez moi/nous …	At my/our house …
on fête (Noël/Divali, etc.)	we celebrate (Christmas/ Diwali, etc.)
on boit du champagne	we drink champagne
on décore le sapin de Noël	we decorate the Christmas tree
on s'offre des cadeaux	we give each other presents
on ouvre les cadeaux	we open the presents
on chante des chants traditionnels	we sing traditional songs
on allume des bougies	we light candles

24

Module 3 Vocabulaire

on cherche des œufs dans le jardin	we look for eggs in the garden	**Fêter le 14 juillet**	***Celebrating Bastille Day***
On prépare/mange ...	We prepare/eat ...	On va aller au bal.	We're going to go to the dance.
de la dinde rôtie	roast turkey	On va regarder le feu d'artifice.	We're going to watch the fireworks.
des légumes (m)	vegetables	On va s'amuser.	We're going to have fun.
une bûche de Noël au chocolat	a chocolate Yule log	On va inviter ...	We're going to invite ...
des crêpes (f)	crêpes		
une galette des Rois	tart eaten for Epiphany		

Had a look ☐ Nearly there ☐ Nailed it ☐

Félicitations! — ***Congratulations!***
l'anniversaire (m) — *birthday*
le mariage — *wedding, marriage*
la fête — *party*
C'était mon anniversaire. — *It was my birthday.*
J'ai reçu beaucoup de cadeaux. — *I received lots of presents.*
Ma sœur a eu son premier bébé. — *My sister had her first baby.*
Je suis allé(e) au mariage de (ma cousine). — *I went to (my cousin's) wedding.*
Mon frère s'est pacsé avec son compagnon. — *My brother entered into a civil partnership with his partner.*
Il y avait ... — *There was/were ...*
beaucoup d'invités — *lots of guests*
un gâteau spécial — *a special cake*
C'était ... — *It was ...*
génial — *great*

Had a look ☐ Nearly there ☐ Nailed it ☐

Had a look ☐ Nearly there ☐ Nailed it ☐

Un repas spécial — ***A special meal***
Je vais/On va apporter ... — *I am/We are going to bring ...*
du jambon — *ham*
du pâté — *pâté*
du saucisson — *salami*
des baguettes (f) — *baguettes*
des biftecks (m) — *steaks*
des saucisses (f) — *sausages*
des salades composées (f) — *mixed salads*
une salade de riz — *a rice salad*
du concombre — *cucumber*
une laitue — *a lettuce*
des tomates (f) — *tomatoes*
des oignons (m) — *onions*
des poivrons (m) — *peppers*
des champignons (m) — *mushrooms*
des abricots (m) — *apricots*
des framboises (f) — *raspberries*
du raisin — *grapes*
des mini-gâteaux (m) — *mini-cakes*
une tarte aux fruits — *a fruit tart*

Had a look ☐ Nearly there ☐ Nailed it ☐

Les magasins — ***Shops***
le marché — *market*
le supermarché — *supermarket*
la boucherie — *butcher's*
la boulangerie — *bakery, baker's*
la charcuterie — *pork butcher's, delicatessen*
la pâtisserie — *cake shop, pastry shop*
l'épicerie (f) — *greengrocer's*

Had a look ☐ Nearly there ☐ Nailed it ☐

M 3

Extra words I should know for reading and listening activities

On fait du shopping! / Let's go shopping!

Ça me déstresse!*	It de-stresses me!
Vous désirez?	How can I help you?
Avez-vous … ?	Have you got … ?
Ça fait combien?	How much is that?
Je prends …	I'll have …
Je suis désolé(e) …	I'm sorry …
Je n'en ai plus.	I haven't got any more.
Alors …	Well/So …
Bien sûr.	Of course.
Ça fait (huit) euros, s'il vous plaît.	That's (eight) euros, please.

Had a look ☐ Nearly there ☐ Nailed it ☐

Les fêtes en France / Festivals/Parties in France

On colle un poisson dans le dos de quelqu'un.**	We stick a fish onto someone's back.
On dit («Poisson d'avril!»).**	We say ("April Fool's Day!").
On mange …	We eat …
Comme dessert …	As a dessert …
J'adore/J'aime fêter mon anniversaire.	I love/like celebrating my birthday.
Je reçois beaucoup de cadeaux.	I get lots of presents.
À part (Noël) …	Apart from (Christmas) …
Je suis né(e) (en août).	I was born (in August).
Le jour de (mon anniversaire) …	The day of (my birthday) …
C'est l'occasion de dire merci à (sa maman).	It's the time to say thank you to (your mum).
Je suis (très) romantique.	I am (very) romantic.
Une de mes fêtes préférées, c'est …	One of my favourite festivals is …
J'aime m'habiller bien.	I like to dress well.
le compte à rebours	the countdown
Tout le monde s'embrasse.*	Everyone kisses each other.

Had a look ☐ Nearly there ☐ Nailed it ☐

Un repas spécial / A special meal

Je vais m'occuper (du dessert).	I'll take care of (the dessert).
Je viens!	I'm coming!
Je vais chercher (le pain).	I'm going to get (the bread).
Je vais faire cuire (des morceaux de poulet).	I'm going to cook (chicken pieces).
Compte sur nous!	Count on us!
On va préparer/boire …	We are going to prepare/drink …
On va acheter à boire!	We are going to buy the drinks.
Des (grandes) bouteilles de …	(Big) bottles of …
On mange chez mes grands-parents/nous.	We eat at my grandparents' house/our house.
Cette année/fois …	This year/time …
Je vais inviter toute ma famille (à un barbecue).	I'm going to invite all of my family (to a barbecue).
La ville où on habite …	The town where we live …
Je (ne) peux (pas) aller au supermarché.	I can('t) go to the supermarket.
Je dois acheter les provisions dans des magasins indépendants.	I have to get the food from small/independent shops.
Avec ça, je vais servir …	I'm going to serve … with that.

Had a look ☐ Nearly there ☐ Nailed it ☐

Felicitations! / Congratulations!

Il y avait beaucoup d'invités.	There were lots of people invited.
J'ai pris des photos.	I took some photos.
la cérémonie	the ceremony
le vin d'honneur	drinks reception
un croquembouche**	special (wedding) cake, made of profiteroles and cream
J'ai fêté …	I celebrated …
C'était une (excellente) soirée!	It was a (great) night!

Had a look ☐ Nearly there ☐ Nailed it ☐

---

*Use cognates/near cognates to work out new words and phrases such as *Ça me déstresse!* or *Tout le monde s'embrasse!*

**Some French customs are different to English ones, such as the cake served at weddings. Make a list in French and English and learn them.

Module 4 Vocabulaire

Words I should know for speaking and writing activities

Où habites-tu?
Where do you live?

J'habite … *I live …*
dans une ville/un village *in a town/village*
au centre-ville *in the town centre*
au bord de la mer *at the seaside*
à la campagne/montagne *in the countryside/mountains*
en ville *in town*
à Londres/Manchester, etc. *in London/Manchester, etc.*
dans le nord/le sud/l'est/l'ouest … *in the north/south/east/west …*
dans le centre … *in the centre …*
de l'Angleterre/Écosse/Irlande (du Nord) *of England/Scotland/(Northern) Ireland*
de la France *of France*
du pays de Galles *of Wales*

Had a look ☐ Nearly there ☐ Nailed it ☐

Qu'est-ce qu'on peut faire?
What can you do?

On peut … *You can …*
aller à un match de foot *go to a football match*
aller au cinéma *go to the cinema*
faire du cheval *go horse-riding*
faire du ski *go skiing*
faire du snowboard *go snowboarding*
faire des promenades *go for walks*
faire les magasins *go shopping*
se baigner dans la mer *swim/bathe in the sea*
se détendre sur la plage *relax on the beach*
visiter le château *visit the castle*
visiter les musées *visit the museums*

Had a look ☐ Nearly there ☐ Nailed it ☐

Dans ma ville/mon village
In my town/village

Dans ma ville/mon village, il y a … *In my town/village, there is/are …*
un bureau de poste/une poste *a post office*
un centre de loisirs *a leisure centre*
un château *a castle*
un marché *a market*
un musée *a museum*
un parc/jardin public *a park*
un stade *a stadium*
un supermarché *a supermarket*
une bibliothèque *a library*
une église *a church*
une gare (SNCF) *a (railway) station*
une mosquée *a mosque*
des hôtels (m) *some hotels*
des restaurants (m) *some restaurants*
Il n'y a pas de … *There isn't a/aren't any …*

Had a look ☐ Nearly there ☐ Nailed it ☐

Les directions
Directions

Où est le/la/l' … ? *Where is the … ?*
Où sont les … ? *Where are the … ?*
Pour aller au/à la/à l'/aux … ? *How do I get to the … ?*
Va/Allez tout droit. *Go straight on.*
Tourne/Tournez à gauche/droite. *Turn left/right.*
Prends/Prenez la première/deuxième/troisième rue à gauche/droite. *Take the first/second/third street on the left/right.*
Traverse/Traversez le pont/la place. *Cross the bridge/square.*
Descends/Descendez la rue. *Go down the street.*
C'est près/loin? *Is it near/far?*
C'est tout près/assez loin. *It's very near/quite far.*

Had a look ☐ Nearly there ☐ Nailed it ☐

Qu'est-ce qu'il y a dans ta région?
What is there in your region?

Dans ma région, il y a … *In my region there is/are …*
un lac *a lake*
un port de pêche *a fishing port*
une rivière/un fleuve *a river*
des champs (m) *fields*
des collines (f) *hills*
des fermes (f) *farms*
des forêts (f) *forests*
des stations de ski (f) *ski resorts*
des vignobles (m) *vineyards*
En Bretagne, il y a … *In Brittany there is/are …*
un beau château *a beautiful castle*
une belle cathédrale *a beautiful cathedral*
des villes historiques *historical towns*
de vieilles maisons *old houses*
de vieux bâtiments *old buildings*
On peut … *You can …*
faire de la voile *go sailing*
faire des randonnées à vélo *go for bike rides*

Had a look ☐ Nearly there ☐ Nailed it ☐

Le meilleur …
The best …

le meilleur climat *the best climate*
la meilleure équipe de football *the best football team*

M
4

27

Module 4 Vocabulaire

le plus beau paysage	the most beautiful countryside	Avez-vous un dépliant/ un plan de la ville?	Do you have a leaflet/a map of the town?
les plus belles plages	the most beautiful beaches	Où est-ce qu'on peut acheter des billets?	Where can we buy tickets?
le plus long fleuve	the longest river	la durée	duration
la plus longue piste de ski	the longest ski slope	les tarifs (m)	prices
		gratuit(e)	free
la plus haute tour	the highest tower	accessible aux personnes handicapées	accessible to disabled people
le musée le plus populaire	the most popular museum	les chiens sont acceptés	dogs are welcome
la région la plus historique	the most historical region		

Had a look ☐   Nearly there ☐   Nailed it ☐

les stations de ski (f) les plus populaires	the most popular ski resorts	**Le temps/La météo**	**The weather/The weather forecast**
les monuments (m) les plus célèbres	the most famous monuments	Quel temps fait-il?	What is the weather like?
		Il fait beau.	The weather is good.

Had a look ☐   Nearly there ☐   Nailed it ☐

Il fait mauvais. — The weather is bad.
Il fait chaud. — It's hot.

Visiter une ville / Visiting a town

Je voudrais visiter/voir …	I would like to visit/see …
Je ne voudrais pas rater …	I wouldn't want to miss …
l'aquarium (m)	the aquarium
l'exposition (f) sur …	the exhibition on …
le spectacle son et lumière	the sound and light show
Je voudrais louer des vélos.	I would like to hire bikes.
J'aimerais …	I would like …
faire une promenade en bateau	to go on a boat trip
monter à la tour de l'horloge	to climb the clock tower

Il fait froid. — It's cold.
Il y a du soleil. — It's sunny.
Il y a du brouillard. — It's foggy.
Il y a du vent. — It's windy.
Il y a un orage. — There's a storm.
Il pleut. — It's raining.
Il neige. — It's snowing.
près de la Manche — near the Channel
sur la côte atlantique — on the Atlantic coast
sur la côte méditerranéenne — on the Mediterranean coast

Had a look ☐   Nearly there ☐   Nailed it ☐

Les projets / Plans

aujourd'hui	today
demain	tomorrow
après-demain	the day after tomorrow
ce week-end	this weekend
cette semaine	this week
S'il fait beau/mauvais (etc.), on va …	If the weather's good/bad (etc.), we're going …
aller à la pêche	to go fishing
aller à la piscine (en plein air)	to go to the (open-air) swimming pool
faire un barbecue	to have a barbecue
faire un pique-nique	to have a picnic
faire de la luge	to go tobogganing
rester à la maison	to stay at home
regarder la télé	to watch TV

Had a look ☐   Nearly there ☐   Nailed it ☐

Had a look ☐   Nearly there ☐   Nailed it ☐

Les renseignements touristiques / Tourist information

(Le château) est ouvert quels jours de la semaine?	On what days is (the castle) open?
C'est ouvert (tous les jours/tous les jours sauf le dimanche).	It's open (every day/every day except Sundays).
Quels sont les horaires d'ouverture?	What are the opening hours?
C'est ouvert de (9h) à (17h).	It's open from (9 a.m.) until (5 p.m.).
C'est combien, l'entrée?	How much is the entrance fee?
Ça coûte … pour les adultes et … pour les enfants.	It costs … for adults and … for children.
Est-ce qu'il y a un restaurant ou une cafétéria?	Is there a restaurant or a cafeteria?

Ville de rêve ou ville de cauchemar? / Dream town or nightmare town?

C'est …	It's …
très animé	very lively
trop tranquille	too quiet

28

Module 4 Vocabulaire

sale	*dirty*
pollué(e)	*polluted*
triste	*sad*
Ce n'est jamais propre.	*It's never clean.*
Il y a …	*There is/are …*
de bons transports en commun	*good public transport*
seulement des maisons et une église	*only houses and a church*
trop de circulation	*too much traffic*
trop de bruit	*too much noise*
toujours des déchets par terre	*always rubbish on the ground*
Il n'y a rien pour les jeunes.	*There is nothing for young people.*
Il n'y a pas grand-chose à faire.	*There is not much to do.*
Il n'y a pas de zone piétonne.	*There is no pedestrian precinct.*
Il n'y a plus de cinéma.	*There is no longer a cinema.*
Le cinéma est fermé.	*The cinema is closed (down).*
un club pour les jeunes	*a youth club*
les poubelles (f)	*bins*
en banlieue	*in the suburbs*
le quartier	*neighbourhood, district, part of town*

Had a look ☐ **Nearly there** ☐ **Nailed it** ☐

Module 4 Vocabulaire

Extra words I should know for reading and listening activities

Qu'est-ce qu'il y a où tu habites?	What is there where you live?	C'est comment où tu habites?	What is it like where you live?
des belles plages	beautiful beaches	tout** ...	very ...
des beaux châteaux	beautiful castles	... petit	... small
des grandes forêts	large forests	... propre	... clean
la capitale	the capital	... triste	... sad
la plus haute montagne de France*	the highest mountain in France	culturel(le)	cultural
le plus grand château de France et du monde*	The biggest castle in France and the world	mon quartier	my neighbourhood
		Il (n')y a ... (rien) pour les jeunes.	There is ... (nothing) for young people.
la meilleure équipe de foot*	The best football team	Il y avait ...	There used to be ...
		un endroit sans pollution	a place without pollution

Had a look ☐   Nearly there ☐   Nailed it ☐

		complètement	completely
Les renseignements touristiques	**Tourist information**	J'ai repondu à un sondage en ligne.	I answered an online survey.
Ça, c'est plus intéressant!	That's more interesting!	les aspects de la ville	the aspects of the town
		Il faut avoir ...	You should have ...
le spectacle son et lumière	sound and lights show	Je veux habiter (dans) un endroit propre.	I want to live in a clean place.
une promenade (commentée) en bateau	(guided) boat trip		

Had a look ☐   Nearly there ☐   Nailed it ☐

une randonnée à vélo	bike ride
les requins (m)	sharks
les navettes spatiales (f)	space shuttles
environ	about
l'horloge (f)	clock tower

Had a look ☐   Nearly there ☐   Nailed it ☐

Les activités	**Activities**
dans le jardin	in the garden
pendant les vacances	during the holidays

Had a look ☐   Nearly there ☐   Nailed it ☐

---

*Learn key geographical, cultural or historical aspects about France, such as which is the longest river, the highest mountain, etc. You can use them in the speaking exam to impress the examiner. This knowledge will also help you understand more easily passages in the reading and listening exams.

**Be very careful of words that can have more than one meaning. *Tout* can mean 'all', 'quite', 'every', 'any' and 'very'!

Another example is *de*, which depending on the context means 'from', 'of', 'some' and 'in'.

Words I should know for speaking and writing activities

Les pays / *Countries*
le Danemark / *Denmark*
le Pakistan / *Pakistan*
le pays de Galles / *Wales*
le Royaume-Uni / *the UK*
l'Algérie (f) / *Algeria*
l'Allemagne (f) / *Germany*
l'Angleterre (f) / *England*
l'Autriche (f) / *Austria*
la Belgique / *Belgium*
l'Espagne (f) / *Spain*
l'Italie (f) / *Italy*
la Pologne / *Poland*
la Russie / *Russia*
la Suisse / *Switzerland*
les États-Unis (m) / *the USA*
les Pays-Bas (m) / *the Netherlands*

Had a look ☐ Nearly there ☐ Nailed it ☐

Les vacances / *Holidays*
Où vas-tu en vacances? / *Where do you go on holiday?*
Je vais … / *I go …*
en France / *to France*
au pays de Galles / *to Wales*
aux États-Unis / *to the USA*
Comment voyages-tu? / *How do you travel?*
Je voyage … / *I travel …*
en avion / *by plane*
en bateau / *by boat*
en car / *by coach*
en train / *by train*
en voiture / *by car*
à vélo / *by bike*
Où loges-tu? / *Where do you stay?*
Je loge dans … / *I stay in/on …*
un camping / *a campsite*
un hôtel / *a hotel*
une auberge de jeunesse / *a youth hostel*
une caravane / *a caravan*

Had a look ☐ Nearly there ☐ Nailed it ☐

Avec qui pars-tu en vacances? / *Who do you go on holiday with?*
Je pars … / *I go …*
avec ma famille / *with my family*
avec mes copains/copines / *with my friends*
avec mes grands-parents / *with my grandparents*
seul(e) / *alone*
C'est comment? / *What's it like?*
C'est … / *It's …*

extra/formidable / *amazing/great*
bien / *good*
ennuyeux/nul / *boring/rubbish*
Ce n'est pas mal. / *It's not bad.*

Had a look ☐ Nearly there ☐ Nailed it ☐

Les hôtels / *Hotels*
un hôtel / *a hotel*
des chambres d'hôtes / *guest rooms (i.e. in a B&B/guest house)*
Nous proposons des chambres avec … / *We offer rooms with …*
un grand lit / *a double bed*
un lit simple / *a single bed*
une salle de bains / *a bathroom*
une douche / *a shower*
un micro-ondes / *a microwave*
une télévision à écran plat / *a flat-screen TV*
(une) vue sur la mer / *a sea view*
un balcon / *a balcony*
la climatisation / *air conditioning*

Had a look ☐ Nearly there ☐ Nailed it ☐

Nous avons aussi … / *We also have …*
une aire de jeux / *a games area*
un parking / *a car park*
une piscine / *a swimming pool*
un restaurant / *a restaurant*
le Wi-Fi / *Wi-Fi*
Nos chambres sont bien équipées. / *Our rooms are well equipped.*
Le petit-déjeuner est inclus/compris. / *Breakfast is included.*
Notre hôtel est situé/se trouve … / *Our hotel is located …*

Had a look ☐ Nearly there ☐ Nailed it ☐

Réserver une chambre / *Booking a room*
Nous voulons/Je voudrais réserver une chambre … / *We want/I would like to book a room …*
pour une/deux personne(s) / *for one person/two people*
avec un lit simple/un grand lit / *with a single/double bed*
pour une nuit/deux nuits / *for one night/two nights*
Est-ce que vous avez … ? / *Do you have … ?*
une piscine / *a swimming pool*
la climatisation / *air conditioning*
Votre chambre est … / *Your room is …*

Module 5 Vocabulaire

au rez-de-chaussée	on the ground floor
au premier étage	on the first floor
au deuxième étage	on the second floor
Je voudrais payer avec ma carte bancaire.	I would like to pay with my debit/credit card.

Had a look ☐ Nearly there ☐ Nailed it ☐

Voyager / Travelling

l'aéroport (m)	airport
le billet	ticket
le conducteur/la conductrice	driver
le contrôle des passeports	passport control
le guichet	ticket office/counter
le/la pilote	pilot
le quai	platform
l'autoroute (f)	motorway
la ceinture de sécurité	seatbelt
la circulation	traffic
la douane	customs
la gare	station
la route	road
les bagages (m)	luggage

Had a look ☐ Nearly there ☐ Nailed it ☐

Au guichet / At the ticket counter

Je peux vous aider?	Can I help you?
Je voudrais un aller simple/un aller-retour pour (Lyon), s'il vous plaît.	I would like a single/a return to (Lyon), please.
En quelle classe?	In which class?
En première/deuxième classe.	In first/second class.
C'est quel quai?	Which platform is it?
Le train part à quelle heure?	What time does the train leave?
Le voyage dure combien de temps?	How long does the journey last?
Est-ce qu'il faut changer?	Do I/we have to change?
C'est un train direct.	The train is direct.

Had a look ☐ Nearly there ☐ Nailed it ☐

Moyens de transports préférés et raisons / Favourite means of transport and reasons

Je voyage toujours (en train, etc.) parce que c'est …	I always travel (by train, etc.) because it's …
plus rapide/plus confortable	faster/more comfortable
plus pratique/plus vert	more practical/greener
plus aventureux	more adventurous
mieux/meilleur pour la planète	better for the planet
moins ennuyeux/fatigant	less boring/tiring
moins cher	less expensive

Had a look ☐ Nearly there ☐ Nailed it ☐

Les activités en vacances / Holiday activities

Je fais de la planche à voile.	I go windsurfing.
Je fais de la voile.	I go sailing.
Je fais de l'accrobranche.	I do a tree-top adventure.
Je fais du ski.	I go skiing.
Je visite les musées.	I visit the museums.
Je visite les monuments.	I visit the monuments.
Je vais à la pêche.	I go fishing.
Je vais à la plage.	I go to the beach.
Je joue à la pétanque.	I play French bowls.
Je me baigne.	I swim (in the sea).
Je me promène.	I go for a walk.
Je me repose.	I rest.
Je me lève (tôt/tard).	I get up (early/late).
Je m'habille.	I get dressed.
Je ne m'ennuie pas.	I don't get bored.
Je sors au restaurant.	I go out to a restaurant.

Had a look ☐ Nearly there ☐ Nailed it ☐

Au restaurant / At the restaurant

Voici la carte.	Here is the menu.
Le plat du jour, c'est …	The daily special is …
Vous avez fait votre choix?	Have you made your choice?
Pour commencer, je vais prendre …	To start, I am going to have …
Comme plat principal, je voudrais …	As a main course, I would like …
Je vais prendre le menu (à 30 euros).	I am going to have the (30 euro) set menu.
Et comme boisson?	And to drink?
Qu'est-ce que vous avez comme desserts?	What desserts do you have?
Vous avez besoin d'autre chose?	Do you need anything else?
On a besoin de l'addition.	We need the bill.
J'ai faim.	I am hungry.
J'ai soif.	I am thirsty.
J'ai envie d'un dessert.	I want a dessert.

Had a look ☐ Nearly there ☐ Nailed it ☐

Les plats / Dishes

les entrées (f)	starters
les brochettes (f) de crevettes (f)	prawn skewers
les escargots (m)	snails
la soupe à la tomate	tomato soup

Module 5 Vocabulaire

la tarte à l'oignon	onion tart	**Des vacances catastrophiques**	***Catastrophic holidays***
les plats principaux (m)	*main dishes*	J'ai oublié mon passeport.	*I forgot my passport.*
l'épaule d'agneau (f)	*shoulder of lamb*	J'ai pris un coup de soleil.	*I got sunburnt.*
la cuisse de canard	*duck leg*	J'ai cassé mon appareil photo.	*I broke my camera.*
les lasagnes végétariennes (f)	*vegetarian lasagne*	J'ai été malade.	*I got sick.*
le loup de mer	*sea bass*	On m'a volé mon sac.	*Someone stole my handbag.*
le poulet basquaise	*Basque-style chicken*	Il a plu tous les jours.	*It rained every day.*
le rôti de veau	*roast veal*	Il y avait des cafards dans notre chambre.	*There were cockroaches in our room.*
les desserts (m)	*desserts*	J'ai raté l'avion.	*I missed the plane.*
la crème brûlée	*crème brûlée*	J'ai dû aller chez le médecin.	*I had to go to the doctor.*
la mousse au chocolat	*chocolate mousse*	J'ai perdu mes photos.	*I lost my photos.*
le roulé au chocolat	*chocolate roll*	J'ai vomi.	*I vomited.*
le sorbet	*sorbet*	J'ai dû aller au commissariat.	*I had to go to the police station.*
la tarte au citron	*lemon tart*	Il n'y avait rien à faire.	*There was nothing to do.*
la tarte aux pommes	*apple tart*	On a dû chercher un autre hôtel.	*We had to look for another hotel.*
l'eau gazeuse (f)	*sparkling water*	La prochaine fois, je vais …	*Next time, I am going …*

Had a look ☐ **Nearly there** ☐ **Nailed it** ☐

Critiques	***Reviews***
J'y suis allé(e) pour le déjeuner/le dîner.	*I went there for lunch/dinner.*
Le service était lent/exceptionnel.	*The service was slow/exceptional.*
Le serveur/La serveuse était/n'était pas (très) poli(e).	*The waiter/waitress was/wasn't (very) polite.*
C'était …	*It was …*
délicieux/bien cuit.	*delicious/well-cooked.*
La nourriture était froide/trop salée.	*The food was cold/too salty.*
La nourriture n'était pas cuite.	*The food wasn't cooked.*
Je recommande/Je ne recommande pas ce restaurant.	*I recommend/don't recommend this restaurant.*

faire plus attention — *to be more careful*
mettre de la crème solaire — *to put on sun cream*
loger dans un camping — *to stay on a campsite*

Had a look ☐ **Nearly there** ☐ **Nailed it** ☐

Had a look ☐ **Nearly there** ☐ **Nailed it** ☐

Module 5 Vocabulaire

Extra words I should know for reading and listening activities

L'hébergement / *Accommodation*

un hôtel familial/de luxe	*a family/luxury hotel by the river*
au bord du fleuve	
un hôtel 4 étoiles prêt à vous accueillir	*a four-star hotel ready to welcome you*
spacieux/-euse(s)	*spacious*
notre maison	*our house*
au premier/deuxième étage	*on the first/second floor*
un parking à votre disposition	*a car park for you*
tout de suite	*straightaway*
une salle de bains privée	*a private bathroom*
une piscine extérieure	*an outdoor swimming pool*
toutes les formules possibles	*all possible options*
une aire de jeux	*a play area*
confortable/parfait	*comfortable/perfect*
Nous mettons …	*We put …*
Nous proposons …	*We offer …*
Nous avons une chambre pour … personnes(s).	*We have a room for … people.*
bien situé(e)	*well-situated*
dormir	*to sleep*
ouvert(e)/fermé(e) toute l'année	*open/closed all year*

Had a look ☐ Nearly there ☐ Nailed it ☐

Pour réserver un hôtel / *To reserve a hotel*

(Comment) voulez-vous (payer)?	*(How) do you want (to pay)?*
Quelle sorte de … ?	*What type of … ?*
Combien de nuits?	*How many nights?*

Had a look ☐ Nearly there ☐ Nailed it ☐

En route! / *On the road!*

(Le train) arrive à quelle heure?	*What time does (the train) arrive?*
Bon voyage!	*Have a good trip!*
Je vais (aller) …*	*I go/am going (to go) …*
J'y vais …	*I go there …*
J'aime (beaucoup) …	*I (really) like …*
prendre l'avion	*to take the plane*
(y) aller en ferry	*to go by ferry*
rencontrer des gens	*to meet people*
voyager en voiture	*to travel by car*
faire du vélo	*to go cycling*
C'est tout simplement la classe!	*It's simply awesome!*
Quand y vas-tu?	*When do you go?*
tous les ans	*every year*
le lendemain	*the day after tomorrow*
C'est (nettement) mieux.	*It's (clearly) better.*

en (juillet)	*in (July)*
Que fais-tu?	*What do you do?*

Had a look ☐ Nearly there ☐ Nailed it ☐

Les vacances de l'année dernière / *Last year's holidays*

C'était mon premier/dernier jour de vacances.	*It was my first/last day of the holidays.*
J'ai décidé de …	*I decided to …*
Je me suis levé(e) …	*I got up …*
très tôt	*very early*
tard	*late*
à midi	*at midday*
Je suis allé(e) …	*I went …*
à la plage	*to the beach*
en boîte	*to a nightclub*
J'ai retrouvé des amis …	*I met friends …*
J'ai vu le lever du soleil.	*I saw the sunrise.*
J'ai dansé au soleil/sous le soleil.	*I danced in the sun.*
Qu'est-ce que c'était beau!	*How beautiful it was!*

Had a look ☐ Nearly there ☐ Nailed it ☐

Bon appétit! / *Enjoy your food!*

Pour commencer, je vais prendre …	*To start, I am going to have …*
Pour moi …	*For me …*
J'ai (très) faim.	*I'm (very) hungry.*
Vous avez besoin d'autre chose?	*Would you like anything else?*
L'addition, s'il vous plaît.	*The bill, please.*
C'était froid/parfait/délicieux.	*It was cold/perfect/delicious.*

Had a look ☐ Nearly there ☐ Nailed it ☐

Les catastrophes! / *Catastrophes!*

Quel dommage!	*What a shame!*
J'ai passé une nuit dans un hôtel sale.	*I spent a night in a dirty hotel.*
Il y avait une odeur bizarre.	*There was a strange smell.*
La salle de bains n'était pas propre non plus!	*The bathroom wasn't clean either!*
La climatisation était cassée.	*The air conditionning was broken.*

Had a look ☐ Nearly there ☐ Nailed it ☐

⭐ *Je fais …* and *Je vais …* can both be translated as 'I go …'. However, you can only use *Je vais …* to mean 'I go …' with a destination. *Je fais …* only means 'I go …' when it is with a sport, for example: *Je fais de la natation.* I go swimming.

Module 6 Vocabulaire

Words I should know for speaking and writing activities

Les matières	*School subjects*
le commerce	business studies
le dessin	art
le français	French
la biologie	biology
la chimie	chemistry
la géographie	geography
la musique	music
la physique	physics
la religion	religious studies
la technologie	technology
l'allemand (m)	German
l'anglais (m)	English
l'art dramatique (m)	drama
le théâtre	drama
l'EPS (f)/le sport	PE
l'espagnol (m)	Spanish
l'étude des médias (f)	media studies
l'histoire (f)	history
l'informatique (f)	ICT
l'instruction civique (f)	citizenship
les arts ménagers (m)	home technology
les maths (m)	maths

Had a look ☐ Nearly there ☐ Nailed it ☐

L'emploi du temps	*The timetable*
à neuf heures	at nine o'clock
à neuf heures dix	at ten past nine
à neuf heures et quart	at a quarter past nine
à neuf heures et demie	at half past nine
à dix heures moins vingt	at twenty to ten
à dix heures moins le quart	at a quarter to ten
lundi	(on) Monday(s)
mardi	(on) Tuesday(s)
mercredi	(on) Wednesday(s)
jeudi	(on) Thursday(s)
vendredi	(on) Friday(s)
la récré(ation)	break time
l'heure du déjeuner	lunchtime
Lundi à neuf heures, j'ai histoire.	On Monday at nine o'clock, I have history.
Vendredi, j'ai deux heures de français.	I have two French lessons on Fridays.
La récré commence à …	Break time starts at …

Had a look ☐ Nearly there ☐ Nailed it ☐

Ce que j'aime et ce que je n'aime pas	*What I like and what I don't like*
Ma matière préférée est …	My favourite subject is …
Je suis fort(e) en …	I am good at …
Je suis faible en …	I am weak at …
Je (ne) suis (pas) doué(e) en …	I (don't) have a talent for …

C'est …	It's …
facile/difficile	easy/difficult
utile/inutile	useful/useless
intéressant/ennuyeux	interesting/boring
fascinant/passionnant	fascinating/exciting
Le/La prof est …	The teacher is …
bon(ne)/marrant(e)	good/funny
sympa/gentil(le)	nice/kind
sévère/impatient(e)	strict/impatient
On a trop de devoirs.	We have too much homework.

Had a look ☐ Nearly there ☐ Nailed it ☐

Une école bien équipée	*A well-equipped school*
le gymnase	sports hall
le hall	(assembly) hall, auditorium
le terrain de basket	basketball court
le terrain de sport	sports ground
la bibliothèque	library
la cantine	canteen
la cour de récréation	playground
la piscine	swimming pool
la salle de sport	gym
les labos de science (m)	science labs
les salles de classe (f)	classrooms
les vestiaires (m)	changing rooms

Had a look ☐ Nearly there ☐ Nailed it ☐

Mon collège	*My school*
Comment s'appelle ton école?	What is your school called?
Mon école s'appelle …	My school is called …
C'est quelle sorte d'école?	What sort of school is it?
C'est …	It's …
une école mixte	a mixed school
une école publique	a state school
une école privée	a private school
une école pour filles/garçons	a school for girls/boys
pour les élèves de 11 à 16 ans	for pupils aged 11 to 16
Il y a combien d'élèves?	How many pupils are there?
Il y a (750) élèves et (45) professeurs.	There are (750) pupils and (45) teachers.
Quels sont les horaires?	What are the school hours?
La journée commence à (8h30) et finit à (16h ou à 17h).	The school day starts at (8.30 a.m.) and finishes at (4 or 5 p.m.).
Il y a combien de cours par jour?	How many lessons are there per day?
Il y a (huit) cours par jour.	There are (eight) lessons per day.

M 6

35

Module 6 Vocabulaire

Comment sont les professeurs?	What are the teachers like?
En général, les profs sont gentils/un peu sévères.	In general, teachers are kind/a bit strict.
Qu'est-ce que tu penses de ton collège?	What do you think of your school?
Je pense que les journées sont longues et qu'on a trop de contrôles.	I think the days are long and we have too many tests.

Had a look ☐ Nearly there ☐ Nailed it ☐

L'école chez nous, l'école chez vous / School here and with you

En Grande-Bretagne, …	In Britain …
En France, …	In France …
l'école commence à … et finit à …	school starts at … and finishes at …
on porte un uniforme scolaire	we wear school uniform
ils portent leurs propres habits	they wear their own clothes
on étudie la religion	we study RE
ils n'étudient pas la religion	they don't study RE
on ne redouble pas	we don't repeat a year
ils redoublent	they repeat a year
les grandes vacances durent …	the summer holidays last …
Je préfère le système britannique/français parce que …	I prefer the British/French system because …
le redoublement (n')est (pas) une bonne idée	repeating a year is (not) a good idea
les horaires sont plus raisonnables	the hours are more reasonable
les vacances sont plus longues	the holidays are longer
l'uniforme scolaire est pratique	school uniform is practical

Had a look ☐ Nearly there ☐ Nailed it ☐

Le règlement scolaire / School rules

Il faut être à l'heure.	You must be on time.
Il faut faire ses devoirs.	You have to do your homework.
Il faut porter l'uniforme scolaire.	You have to wear school uniform.
Il est interdit de mâcher du chewing-gum.	It is forbidden to chew gum.
Il est interdit d'utiliser son portable en classe.	It is forbidden to use your mobile phone in class.
Il est interdit de porter des bijoux, des piercings ou trop de maquillage.	It is forbidden to wear jewellery, piercings or too much make-up.
Il est interdit de sortir de l'école pendant l'heure du déjeuner.	It is forbidden to leave school at lunchtime.
Il est interdit de manquer les cours.	It is forbidden to skip lessons.
Je trouve ça … juste/logique raisonnable/frustrant(e) injuste/ridicule	I think that's … fair/logical reasonable/frustrating unfair/ridiculous

Had a look ☐ Nearly there ☐ Nailed it ☐

parce que/car …	because …
c'est/ce n'est pas dangereux	it is/isn't dangerous
c'est/ce n'est pas important	it is/isn't important
on n'est pas des bébés	we aren't babies
il faut respecter les autres	you have to respect other people
la mode/la religion n'a pas de place à l'école	fashion/religion doesn't have any place in school
l'école, c'est pour apprendre	school is for learning

Had a look ☐ Nearly there ☐ Nailed it ☐

L'uniforme scolaire / School uniform

Je porte …	I wear …
un pantalon/un polo	trousers/a polo shirt
un sweat/une chemise	a sweatshirt/a shirt
une cravate/une jupe	a tie/a skirt
une veste	a blazer/jacket
mes propres vêtements (m)	my own clothes
La mode n'a pas de place à l'école.	Fashion has no place in school.
L'uniforme coûte cher.	Uniform is expensive.
Tout le monde se ressemble.	Everyone looks the same/alike.
C'est démodé et embarrassant.	It's old-fashioned and embarrassing.
C'est pratique et confortable.	It's practical and comfortable.

Had a look ☐ Nearly there ☐ Nailed it ☐

La santé au collège / Health at school

Pour être en pleine forme, …	To be healthy, …
Pour éviter le stress au collège, …	To avoid stress at school, …
je mange sainement	I eat healthily
je mange rarement des bonbons ou des gâteaux	I rarely eat sweets or cakes
je bois uniquement de l'eau	I only drink water
je ne bois jamais de boissons gazeuses	I never drink fizzy drinks

Module 6 Vocabulaire

je me couche tôt	I go to bed early
j'essaie de me déconnecter des écrans de temps en temps	I try to disconnect from screens from time to time

Had a look ☐ Nearly there ☐ Nailed it ☐

Je m'inquiète pour (mon copain/ma sœur).	I am worried about (my friend/my sister).
Il/Elle ...	He/She ...
fume des cigarettes	smokes cigarettes
fume du cannabis	smokes cannabis
boit de l'alcool	drinks alcohol
ne mange pas sainement	doesn't eat healthily
Il/Elle fait ça pour ...	He/She does that ...
s'amuser	to have fun
faire partie du groupe	to be part of a group
combattre le stress au collège	to combat/to deal with stress at school
perdre du poids	to lose weight
Il/Elle ...	He/She ...
est moins sociable	is less sociable
ne peut pas se concentrer en classe	can't concentrate in class
va avoir de mauvaises notes	is going to have bad grades
va devenir anorexique	is going to become anorexic
À mon avis, c'est ...	In my opinion, it's ...
très mauvais pour la santé	very bad for your health
dangereux/illégal	dangerous/illegal
On devient facilement accro.	You become addicted easily.

Had a look ☐ Nearly there ☐ Nailed it ☐

À l'école primaire et maintenant / At primary school and now

J'avais ...	I had/used to have ...
J'ai ...	I have ...
beaucoup de temps libre	lots of free time
beaucoup d'amis	lots of friends
trop de devoirs	too much homework
J'allais ...	I used to go ...
Je vais ...	I go ...
au ciné-club	to film club
au club d'échecs	to chess club
au zoo	to the zoo
à la piscine	to the swimming pool
J'étais ...	I was/used to be ...
Je suis ...	I am ...
dans une chorale	in a choir
délégué(e) de classe	class representative
membre de l'équipe de basket	a member of the basketball team
timide	shy

Had a look ☐ Nearly there ☐ Nailed it ☐

Je faisais ...	I used to do/go ...
Je fais ...	I do/go ...
du judo/du karaté	judo/karate
du yoga/de la danse	yoga/dancing
de la natation	swimming
Je jouais ...	I used to play ...
Je joue ...	I play ...
à cache-cache	hide and seek
au foot/au hand	football/handball
au ping-pong	ping pong, table tennis
au rugby	rugby
Je participais ...	I used to participate/take part ...
Je participe ...	I participate/take part ...
au spectacle de Noël	in the Christmas play
Je chantais ...	I sang ...
Je chante ...	I sing ...
dans la chorale	in the choir

Had a look ☐ Nearly there ☐ Nailed it ☐

Les succès au collège / Successes at school

Je suis fier/-ière de moi.	I am proud of myself.
Je joue dans l'orchestre.	I play in the orchestra.
Je suis membre du club informatique.	I'm a member of the IT club.
Je suis membre du conseil d'administration.	I'm a member of the school council.
Je vais jouer dans l'équipe de hockey.	I'm going to play in the hockey team.
Je vais participer à un échange scolaire.	I'm going to take part in a school exchange.
J'ai gagné ...	I won ...
un prix pour mes efforts en classe	a prize for my efforts in class
le championnat de foot/basket	the football/basketball championship
un concours de slam/danse	a slam/dance competition

Had a look ☐ Nearly there ☐ Nailed it ☐

J'ai participé à ...	I participated/took part in ...
un spectacle	a show
un échange scolaire	a school exchange
une sortie scolaire	a school visit
J'ai organisé ...	I organised ...
un concert	a concert
un concours de chant	a singing competition
J'ai récolté de l'argent pour une association caritative.	I raised money for a charity.
Les sorties scolaires sont une bonne/mauvaise idée parce que/qu' ...	School visits are a good/bad idea because ...
on se fait de nouveaux amis	you make new friends
on s'amuse ensemble	you have a laugh together
c'est trop cher/ennuyeux	it's too expensive/boring

Had a look ☐ Nearly there ☐ Nailed it ☐

M 6

37

Module 6 Vocabulaire

Extra words I should know for reading and listening activities

Mes matières et mes profs — *My subjects and my teachers*
Mon/Ma prof s'appelle … — *My teacher is called …*
Les profs (de maths) sont … — *The (maths) teachers are …*
Je le/la/les déteste. — *I hate him/her/them.*
Je l'/les adore. — *I love him/her/them.*
Je pense que … est (trop/très/assez/un peu) … — *I think that … is (too/very/quite/a little) …*
C'est amusant/excellent. — *It is fun/excellent.*

Had a look ☐ Nearly there ☐ Nailed it ☐

Dans mon collège — *In my school*
Il y a (environ) … — *There is/are (about) …*
Malheureusement, il n'y a pas de … — *Unfortunately, there isn't/aren't …*
des salles de classes modernes (f) — *modern classrooms*
une grande cour de récréation — *a big playground*
un grand choix de … — *a great choice of …*
un labo(ratoire) de langues/sciences — *a language/science laboratory*
un gymnase immense — *a huge gym*
Les vestiaires/les toilettes sont sales/sont pleins de … — *The changing rooms/toilets are dirty/full of …*
Je le/la/les trouve bien/utile(s)/cool/bien aménagé(es). — *I think it is/they are good/useful/cool/well-equipped.*

Had a look ☐ Nearly there ☐ Nailed it ☐

Les études en Angleterre et en France — *Studying in France and in England*
Les cours commencent/finissent à … heure(s). — *Lessons start/end at … o'clock.*
La récré est à … et dure … minutes. — *Break starts at … and lasts … minutes.*
Il y a … cours par jour/élèves/contrôles. — *There are … lessons per day/pupils/tests.*
Il n'y a pas cours le … — *There are no lessons on …*
On a … heure(s) pour le déjeuner. — *We have … hour(s) for lunch.*
On a trop de … — *We have too many …*
Les journées/cours sont (trop) … — *The days/lessons are (too) …*
un lycée — *a high school (Yr 11-13 only)*
En sixième/cinquième/quatrième/troisième/seconde*/première*/terminale* — *In Yr 7/8/9/10/11/12/13*
à l'âge de … ans — *at the age of … years old*

après le collège — *after middle/high school*
S'ils ne font pas assez de progrès, ils redoublent**. — *If they do not make enough progress, they repeat the year.*
Les élèves passent leur brevet du collège/baccalauréat/en classe supérieure. — *The pupils take their GCSEs/A Levels/move up to the next class.*
Les élèves continuent leurs études à l'université. — *The pupils continue their studies at university.*
Les grandes vacances durent … semaines/mois. — *The summer holidays last … weeks/months.*

Had a look ☐ Nearly there ☐ Nailed it ☐

L'uniforme scolaire — *School uniform*
le jean — *jeans*
le jogging — *jogging pants*
le pull — *a jumper*
le tee-shirt — *t-shirt*
La mode/L'uniforme coûte cher. — *Fashion/The uniform is expensive.*
La mode n'a pas de place … — *Fashion has no place …*
se ressembler — *to look like each other*
Je (ne) voudrais (pas) … — *I would (not) like …*
C'est démodé. — *It's old-fashioned.*
C'est pratique. — *It's practical.*
C'est confortable. — *It's confortable.*
C'est embarrassant. — *It's embarrassing.*

Had a look ☐ Nearly there ☐ Nailed it ☐

La vie extra-scolaire — *After-school activities*
l'orchestre (m) — *the orchestra*
faire du théâtre/beaucoup de clubs — *to do drama/lots of clubs*
aller à la piscine municipale — *to go to the local pool*

Had a look ☐ Nearly there ☐ Nailed it ☐

Être en pleine forme — *To be healthy*
J'essaie de manger cinq portions de fruits et légumes. — *I try to eat five portions of fruit and vegetables.*
Je (ne) mange (pas) bien/assez le matin. — *I (don't) eat well/enough in the morning.*
Un bon petit-déjeuner est essentiel. — *A good breakfast is essential.*
Pour éviter le stress … — *To avoid stress …*
Je fais du sport régulièrement. — *I do sport regularly.*

Module 6 Vocabulaire

Quand je dors mal/bien …	When I sleep badly/well …
Avant de dormir …	Before going to bed …
Avant d'aller au collège …	Before going to school …
Je suis (trop) fatigué(e) pour apprendre.	I am (too) tired to learn.

Had a look ☐ Nearly there ☐ Nailed it ☐

Je vais/On va participer au concours de …	I am going/We are going to participate in a … competition.
Je vais/On va voir une pièce de théâtre.	I am going/We are going to see a play.

Had a look ☐ Nearly there ☐ Nailed it ☐

Les soucis / Worries

Il/Elle fume.	He/She smokes.
Il/Elle fait énormement de sport.	He/She does lots of sport.
perdre du poids	to lose weight
J'ai peur!	I'm scared!
Je pense que …	I think that …
Il/Elle a de nouveaux copains/nouvelles copines.	He/She has new friends.
Il/Elle est plus/moins …	He/She is more/less …
Il/Elle va avoir de mauvaises notes*.	He/She is going to get bad grades.

Had a look ☐ Nearly there ☐ Nailed it ☐

Qu'est-ce que tu fais pour ton collège? / What do you do for your school?

Je représente ma classe.	I represent my class.
On discute des problèmes au collège.	We discuss problems at school.
On organise des activités.	We organise activities.
On a organisé un concours de (slam).	We organised a (slam) competition.
On a joué contre une équipe de …	We played against a team from …
On a gagné le match.	We won the match.
J'ai fait/Je vais faire un échange.	I did/I am going to do an exchange.
J'ai parlé …	I spoke …

M6

⭐ *Watch out for false friends such as *seconde*, *première* and *terminale*. In the context of school, all of these words have very specific meanings: Year 11, Year 12 and Year 13.

Learn as many as you can, such as *les notes* (marks/grades), so that you avoid mistranslating phrases.

⭐ **Redoubler* in a school context does not mean 'to redouble'. It conveys the idea of repeating a school year, which is something French pupils have to do if they don't make sufficient progress over the year! It is important that you learn how the French education system works as it is very different to the English one.

Words I should know for speaking and writing activities

Les métiers — *Jobs*
Je suis/Il/Elle est … — *I am/He/She is a/an …*
Je veux être … — *I want to be a/an …*
Je veux travailler comme … — *I want to work as a/an …*
avocat/avocate — *lawyer*
ingénieur/ingénieure — *engineer*
électricien/électricienne — *electrician*
mécanicien/mécanicienne — *mechanic*
musicien/musicienne — *musician*
maçon/maçonne — *builder*
patron/patronne — *boss*
coiffeur/coiffeuse — *hairdresser*
programmeur/programmeuse — *computer programmer*
serveur/serveuse — *waiter/waitress*
vendeur/vendeuse — *salesperson*
acteur/actrice — *actor/actress*
agriculteur/agricultrice — *farmer*
créateur/créatrice de mode — *fashion designer*
créateur/créatrice de jeux vidéo — *video game designer*
directeur/directrice d'entreprise — *company director*
facteur/factrice — *postman/woman*

Had a look ☐ Nearly there ☐ Nailed it ☐

instituteur/institutrice — *primary school teacher*
boucher/bouchère — *butcher*
boulanger/boulangère — *baker*
fermier/fermière — *farmer*
infirmier/infirmière — *nurse*
pompier/pompière — *firefighter*
architecte — *architect*
chef de cuisine — *chef*
comptable — *accountant*
dentiste — *dentist*
journaliste — *journalist*
pilote — *pilot*
secrétaire — *secretary*
vétérinaire — *vet*
agent de police — *policeman/woman*
médecin — *doctor*
professeur — *teacher*
soldat — *soldier*

Had a look ☐ Nearly there ☐ Nailed it ☐

Lieux de travail — *Workplaces*
Je travaille/Il/Elle travaille … — *I work/He/She works …*
dans un bureau — *in an office*
dans un commissariat de police — *in a police station*
dans un collège — *in a secondary school*
dans un garage — *in a garage*
dans un hôpital — *in a hospital*
dans un magasin — *in a shop*
dans un restaurant — *in a restaurant*
dans un salon de coiffure — *in a hair salon*
dans une boulangerie — *in a bakery*
dans une école primaire — *in a primary school*
dans une ferme — *on a farm*
à bord d'un avion — *on a plane*

Had a look ☐ Nearly there ☐ Nailed it ☐

Les passions — *Passions*
Ma passion, c'est … — *My passion is …*
la cuisine/la mode — *cooking/fashion*
le sport/le théâtre — *sport/theatre/drama*
les ordinateurs (m)/les voitures (f) — *computers/cars*

Had a look ☐ Nearly there ☐ Nailed it ☐

J'aimerais … — *I would like to …*
Je voudrais/J'aimerais travailler … — *I would like to work …*
dans un bureau — *in an office*
dans un magasin — *in a shop*
en plein air — *outside*
avec des enfants — *with children*
avec des animaux — *with animals*
avec des ordinateurs — *with computers*
seul(e) — *alone, on my own*
en équipe — *in a team*
à l'étranger — *abroad*
Je voudrais faire un métier … — *I would like to do a … job*
créatif — *creative*
manuel — *manual*
à responsabilité — *responsible, with responsibility/management*

Had a look ☐ Nearly there ☐ Nailed it ☐

Tu voudrais travailler dans quel secteur et pourquoi? — *What area would you like to work in and why?*
Je voudrais travailler dans … — *I would like to work in …*
le sport et les loisirs — *sport and leisure*
le commerce — *business*
la médecine et la santé — *medicine and health*
l'audiovisuel et les médias — *audiovisual and media*

Module 7 Vocabulaire

l'informatique et les télécommunications	IT and telecommunications	Je lave la voiture (de mon père).	I wash the car (my dad's car).
l'hôtellerie et la restauration	the hotel and catering industry	Je tonds la pelouse (de mes grands-parents).	I mow the lawn (my grandparents' lawn).

Had a look ☐ Nearly there ☐ Nailed it ☐

Je promène le chien.	I walk the dog.
J'ai un petit boulot.	I have a part-time job.
Je sers les clients.	I serve customers.
Je suis …	I am …
Je remplis les rayons.	I stack the shelves.
indépendant(e)	independent
Je fais du baby-sitting (pour mes voisins).	I babysit (for my neighbours).
intelligent(e)	intelligent
motivé(e)	motivated
Je livre des journaux.	I deliver newspapers.
(bien) organisé(e)	(well-)organised
Je gagne/Je reçois …	I earn/I receive/get …
actif/-ve	active
Mon père/Ma mère me donne …	My father/mother gives me …
créatif/-ve	creative
ambitieux/-euse	ambitious
Mes parents me donnent …	My parents give me …
sérieux/-euse	serious
travailleur/-euse	hard-working
quinze euros/dix livres …	fifteen euros/ten pounds …
sociable	sociable
timide	shy
… par heure/jour/ semaine/mois	… per hour/day/week/ month
J'aime …	I like …
le contact avec les gens	(having) contact with people
travailler en équipe	working in a team

Had a look ☐ Nearly there ☐ Nailed it ☐

J'aimerais avoir un métier bien payé.	I would like to have a well-paid job.

Had a look ☐ Nearly there ☐ Nailed it ☐

Postuler à un emploi — Applying for a job

une annonce	an advert
on recherche …	we are looking for …
les responsabilités (f)	responsibilities
les qualifications (f)	qualifications
les compétences (f)	skills

Mes projets d'avenir — My plans for the future

Je veux/J'espère/Je voudrais …	I want/I hope/I would like …
l'expérience (f)	experience
les atouts (m)	strengths
remplir un CV	to fill in a CV
passer mes examens	to take my exams
écrire une lettre de motivation	to write a covering letter
réussir mes examens	to pass my exams
prendre une année sabbatique	to take a gap year
faire une vidéo	to make a video

Had a look ☐ Nearly there ☐ Nailed it ☐

voyager/visiter d'autres pays	to travel/to visit other countries

Mon stage — My work experience

faire un apprentissage/ devenir apprenti(e)	to do an apprenticeship/ to become an apprentice
J'ai fait un stage …	I did work experience …
dans un bureau	in an office
dans un garage	in a garage
aller à l'université/ continuer mes études à la fac(ulté)	to go to university/ to continue my studies at university
dans un hôtel	in a hotel
dans un magasin de mode	in a clothes shop
faire du bénévolat/du travail bénévole	to do voluntary work
dans un salon de coiffure	in a hairdressing salon
me marier ou me pacser	to get married or enter into a civil partnership
dans une banque	in a bank
avoir des enfants	to have children
J'ai servi les clients.	I served customers.
habiter/m'installer avec mon copain/ma copine	to live/move in with my boyfriend/girlfriend
J'ai rangé les vêtements.	I tidied the clothes.
J'ai aidé les mécaniciens.	I helped the mechanics.
J'ai appris à changer des pneus.	I learned to change tyres.

Had a look ☐ Nearly there ☐ Nailed it ☐

Gagner de l'argent — Earning money

Tu as un petit boulot?	Do you have a part-time job?
J'ai tapé des documents.	I typed documents.
J'ai fait des photocopies.	I made photocopies.
Que fais-tu pour gagner de l'argent?	What do you do to earn money?
J'ai lavé les cheveux des clients.	I washed customers' hair.
J'aide à la maison.	I help at home.
Je passe l'aspirateur.	I do the vacuuming.
Je fais la vaisselle.	I do the dishes.
J'ai fait du café.	I made coffee.

M 7

41

Module 7 Vocabulaire

J'ai passé l'aspirateur.	I did the vacuuming.
J'ai répondu au téléphone.	I answered the phone.
J'ai fait des réservations.	I made bookings.
J'ai envoyé des e-mails.	I sent emails.

Had a look ☐ **Nearly there** ☐ **Nailed it** ☐

C'était une bonne expérience?
Was it a good experience?

C'était …	It was …
amusant/bien	fun/good
génial/intéressant	great/interesting
passionnant	exciting
une bonne expérience	a good experience
difficile/ennuyeux	difficult/boring
fatigant/monotone	tiring/monotonous
(complètement) nul	(completely) rubbish
une mauvaise expérience	a bad experience
Mon patron/Ma patronne était … gentil(le)/trop sévère.	My boss was … kind/too strict.
Mes collègues (n') étaient (pas) (très) sympa.	My colleagues were (not) (very) nice.
J'ai beaucoup appris.	I learned a lot.
Je n'ai rien appris.	I didn't learn anything.

Had a look ☐ **Nearly there** ☐ **Nailed it** ☐

Module 7 Vocabulaire

Extra words I should know for reading and listening activities

Les qualités personnelles — *Personal qualities*
en bonne forme	*fit*
fort(e)/patient(e)	*strong/patient*
calme/sociable	*calm/sociable*
heureux/-euse	*happy*

Had a look ☐   Nearly there ☐   Nailed it ☐

L'avenir — *The future*
un métier fascinant/passionnant	*a fascinating/exciting job*
Tu peux sauver la vie des gens!	*You can save people's lives!*
Tu peux devenir célèbre!	*You can become famous!*
Pourquoi ne pas devenir … ?*	*Why not become … ?*
Pense à être …	*Think of being …*
Aimerais-tu être … ?*	*Would you like to be … ?*
Je prendrai …	*I will take …*
J'irai …	*I will go …*
J'aurai …	*I will have …*
Je serai …*	*I will be …*
Je trouverai …	*I will find …*
Je me marierai …	*I will get married …*
l'homme/la femme de mes rêves	*the man/woman of my dreams*
ma propre entreprise	*my own business*
le tour du monde**	*tour of the world*
Ce sera génial!	*It will be great!*
le mariage	*the marriage*
la cérémonie	*the ceremony*
l'église (f)	*the church*
mon futur mari/ma future femme	*my future husband/wife*
être marié(e)(s) depuis … ans	*to be married for … years*
habiter ensemble	*to live together*
pour voir si ça marche	*to see if it works out*
fonder une famille	*to start a family*

Had a look ☐   Nearly there ☐   Nailed it ☐

⭐ *Remember not to use an article after a verb (conjugated or in the infinitive form) when you are talking about a job.*

Examples:
Pourquoi ne pas devenir pilote? — Why not become a pilot?
Aimerais-tu être chanteuse? — Would you like to be a singer?
Je serai prof. — I will be a teacher.

Jobs in French usually have masculine and feminine versions of their spellings but not all.

Pour gagner de l'argent … — *To earn money …*
Je fais ça gratuitement.	*I do that for free.*
chaque semaine	*every week*
quand il/elle n'est pas là	*when he/she isn't there*
J'ai déjà un peu d'expérience de …	*I already have a little experience of …*
postuler au poste de …	*to apply for the post/position of …*

Had a look ☐   Nearly there ☐   Nailed it ☐

Les expériences récentes — *Recent experiences*
J'ai travaillé …	*I worked …*
J'ai supervisé …	*I supervised …*
J'ai décidé de …	*I decided to …*
J'ai commencé à …	*I started to …*
Mon travail consiste à …	*My job consists of …*
Les horaires sont (un peu) longs.	*The days/The working hours are (a little) long.*

Had a look ☐   Nearly there ☐   Nailed it ☐

Le service civique — *Civic service*
pour aider les autres	*to help others*
Ça consiste en/à …	*It consists of …*
une période de (six) à (douze) mois	*a period of (six) to (twelve) months*
selon (leurs) centres d'intérêt	*according to (their) interests*
choisir parmi un grand nombre de «missions»	*to choose from a large number of 'missions'*
la culture et les loisirs	*culture and leisure*
l'éducation et la santé	*education and health*
les sports ou l'environnement	*sports or the environment*
le point de départ	*the starting point*
trouver un emploi	*to find a job*
(leur) motivation principale	*(their) main motivation*
faire quelque chose d'utile à la société	*to do something useful for society*
(Le service civique) sera un atout pour (leur) CV.	*(Civic service) will be a strength on (their) CV.*

Had a look ☐   Nearly there ☐   Nailed it ☐

⭐ **Some nouns in French change their meaning, depending on whether they are used in the masculine or feminine form.
le Tour de France the Tour de France (cycle race)
la tour Eiffel the Eiffel Tower

M 7

43

Module 8 Vocabulaire

Words I should know for speaking and writing activities

Ce qui est important pour moi — *What's important to me*

Ce qui est important pour moi, c'est …	What's important to me is …
l'argent (m)	money
le sport	sport
la musique	music
ma famille	my family
ma santé	my health
mes amis (m)	my friends
mes animaux (m)	my animals
mes études (f)	my studies

Had a look ☐ Nearly there ☐ Nailed it ☐

Ce qui me préoccupe — *What concerns me*

Ce qui me préoccupe, c'est …	What concerns me is …
l'environnement (m)	the environment
l'état (m) de la planète	the state of the planet
le racisme	racism
la cruauté envers les animaux	cruelty to animals
la faim	hunger
la guerre	war
l'injustice (f)	injustice
la pauvreté	poverty
la violence	violence

Had a look ☐ Nearly there ☐ Nailed it ☐

Qu'est-ce qu'on peut faire pour aider? — *What can we do to help?*

On peut faire du bénévolat.	You can do voluntary work.
On peut parrainer un enfant.	You can sponsor a child.
On peut donner de l'argent à une association caritative.	You can give money to a charity.
On peut recycler.	You can recycle.
Il faut agir.	You/We have to act.
Il faut lutter contre la faim.	You/We have to fight against hunger.
Il faut signer des pétitions.	You/We have to sign petitions.
Il faut participer à des manifestations.	You/We have to take part in demonstrations.
Il faut éduquer les gens.	You/We have to educate people.

Had a look ☐ Nearly there ☐ Nailed it ☐

Quel temps fera-t-il? — *What will the weather be like?*

Il y aura …	There will be …
de la pluie	rain
de la neige	snow
du vent	wind
du tonnerre	thunder
des averses (f)	showers
des éclairs (m)	lightning
des éclaircies (f)	sunny intervals
Il fera …	It/The weather will be …
beau	nice, good
mauvais	bad
chaud	hot
froid	cold
frais	chilly
Le temps sera …	The weather will be …
ensoleillé	sunny
nuageux	cloudy
orageux	stormy

Had a look ☐ Nearly there ☐ Nailed it ☐

Les problèmes environnementaux — *Environmental problems*

Le plus grand problème environnemental, c'est …	The biggest environmental problem is …
le changement climatique	climate change
le manque d'eau potable	the lack of drinking water
la disparition des espèces	the extinction of species
la destruction des forêts tropicales	the destruction of the rainforests
la surpopulation	overpopulation
la pollution de l'air	air pollution
la sécheresse	drought
les inondations (f)	flooding, floods
les incendies (m)	fires
Les arbres nous donnent de l'oxygène et nous les coupons tous les jours.	Trees give us oxygen, and every day we cut them down.
Beaucoup de personnes n'ont pas accès à cette ressource vitale.	Lots of people don't have access to this vital resource.
On détruit la planète.	We are destroying the planet.
C'est très inquiétant.	It's very worrying.
C'est catastrophique.	It's catastrophic.

Had a look ☐ Nearly there ☐ Nailed it ☐

Que doit-on faire pour sauver notre planète? — *What should we do to save our planet?*

On doit/On peut …	You/We should/can …
recycler	recycle
trier les déchets	separate/sort the rubbish
faire du compost	make compost

Module 8 Vocabulaire

consommer moins d'énergie	consume less energy
éteindre les appareils électriques et la lumière	turn off electrical appliances and the light
mettre un pullover au lieu d'allumer le chauffage	put on a jumper instead of turning on the heating
faire des achats responsables	make responsible purchases
utiliser du papier recyclé	use recycled paper
acheter des produits verts et des produits bio	buy green and organic products

Had a look ☐ Nearly there ☐ Nailed it ☐

voyager autrement	travel differently
utiliser les transports en commun	use public transport
aller au collège à vélo	go to school by bike
réutiliser	reuse
refuser les sacs en plastique	turn down plastic bags
avoir une bouteille d'eau au lieu de prendre un gobelet jetable	have a bottle of water instead of taking a disposable cup
économiser l'eau	save water
boire l'eau du robinet	drink tap water
prendre une douche au lieu de prendre un bain	take a shower instead of a bath
tirer la chasse d'eau moins fréquemment	flush the toilet less frequently
fermer le robinet en se lavant les dents	turn off the tap while brushing your teeth
installer des panneaux solaires	install solar panels

Had a look ☐ Nearly there ☐ Nailed it ☐

D'où vient ton tee-shirt? — *Where does your T-shirt come from?*

Les produits pas chers sont souvent fabriqués dans des conditions de travail inacceptables.	Cheap products are often made in unacceptable working conditions.
Les ouvriers sont sous-payés.	The workers are underpaid.
Leur journée de travail est trop longue.	Their working day is too long.
Il faut/On doit …	We must …
forcer les grandes marques à garantir un salaire minimum	force big brands to guarantee a minimum wage
acheter des produits issus du commerce équitable	buy fair trade products
acheter des vêtements fabriqués en France/au Royaume-Uni	buy clothes that are made in France/in the UK

réfléchir à l'impact sur l'environnement	think about the impact on the environment
essayer de respecter l'homme et l'environnement à la fois	try to respect people and the environment at the same time

Had a look ☐ Nearly there ☐ Nailed it ☐

Faire du bénévolat — *Doing volunteer work*

Tu peux/J'aimerais …	You can/I would like …
travailler avec des personnes âgées	to work with elderly people
travailler avec des enfants	to work with children
travailler avec des sans-abri/des SDF	to work with homeless people
travailler avec des animaux	to work with animals
participer à un projet de conservation	to participate in a conservation project
Je fais du bénévolat parce que …	I do volunteer work because …
pour moi, c'est important d'aider les autres	for me, it's important to help other people
pour moi, c'est important de participer à la vie en société	for me, it's important to participate in society
j'aime développer de nouvelles compétences	I like developing new skills
j'aime rencontrer de nouvelles personnes	I like meeting new people
c'est une expérience enrichissante pour moi	it's a rewarding experience for me
ça me donne plus confiance en moi	it gives me more confidence in myself

Had a look ☐ Nearly there ☐ Nailed it ☐

Je travaille avec …	I work with …
J'aide un enfant avec ses devoirs.	I help a child with his homework.
Je participe à …	I participate in …
Je suis membre de l'organisation …	I am a member of the organisation …
Je travaille dans un refuge.	I work in a refuge/shelter.
Je parle/discute avec …	I talk to …
Je promène les chiens.	I walk the dogs.

Had a look ☐ Nearly there ☐ Nailed it ☐

Les grands événements — *Big events*

Cet événement/Ce genre d'événement …	This event/This type of event …
attire les touristes	attracts tourists

M 8

Module 8 Vocabulaire

encourage la pratique du sport	encourages participation in sport
donne des modèles aux jeunes	gives young people role models
permet aux gens de s'amuser	allows people to have a good time
unit les gens	unites people
L'année dernière/L'été dernier, …	Last year/Last summer, …
je suis allé(e) à un festival/à la Coupe du Monde	I went to a festival/to the World Cup
j'ai vu (le Tour de France)	I saw (the Tour de France)
C'est …	It's …
un événement qui est connu dans le monde entier	an event that is known throughout the world
le plus grand festival (de théâtre) au monde	the biggest (theatre) festival in the world
Il y a une ambiance magique!	There is a magical atmosphere!
Il a lieu/Ça se passe (à Nice/en février).	It takes place (in Nice/in February).
L'été prochain/L'année prochaine, …	Next summer/Next year, …
je vais y retourner	I am going to go back there
je vais aller à …	I am going to go to …
je vais encore regarder …	I am going to watch … again

Had a look ☐ Nearly there ☐ Nailed it ☐

Module 8 Vocabulaire

Extra words I should know for reading and listening activities

Le climat de notre planète — *Our planet's climate*

Il y aura (plus/moins de) soleil/pluie/vent/neige/tempêtes tropicales. — *There will be (more/less) sun/rain/wind/snow/tropical storms.*
un (très violent) cyclone/ouragan* — *a (very violent) cyclone/hurricane*
le changement climatique au cours du XXIe siècle — *climate change over the course of the 21st century*
la température globale — *global temperature*
les conséquences (f) — *the consequences*
causer d'énormes destructions et plusieurs morts — *to cause massive destruction and several deaths*
frapper — *to strike, to hit*
le Pacifique sud — *the southern Pacific Ocean*
contaminer — *to pollute*
une ressource vitale — *a vital resource*
recycler le verre/carton/papier — *to recycle glass/cardboard/paper*
allumer rarement le chauffage — *to rarely put the heating on*
être membre d'une équipe verte — *to be a member of an environmental team*
installer des panneaux solaires — *to put in solar panels*

Had a look ☐   Nearly there ☐   Nailed it ☐

Les produits verts? — *Environmentally friendly products?*

Le coton est cultivé … — *The cotton is grown …*
Le coton est une plante. — *Cotton is a plant.*
Les balles de coton sont transportées/chargées/exportées/transformées/envoyées … en tissu — *The cotton balls are transported/loaded/exported/transformed/sent … into material*
fabriquer dans une usine — *to make in a factory*
repartir pour — *to set off back to*
le motif imprimé(e) — *slogan printed*
Tu portes le tee-shirt pendant un moment … — *You wear the T-shirt for a while …*
Tu donnes le tee-shirt à une association caritative. — *You give the T-shirt to a charity.*
vendu à un prix favorable — *sold at a good price*
les gens dans les pays pauvres — *people in poor countries*
avoir quelque chose de qualité — *to have something of quality*
Évitons la pollution!** — *Let's avoid pollution!*

Had a look ☐   Nearly there ☐   Nailed it ☐

Le bénévolat — *Voluntary work*

planter des arbres — *to plant trees*
le froid — *the cold*
la solitude — *loneliness*

Had a look ☐   Nearly there ☐   Nailed it ☐

Les grands événements — *Big events*

Ce genre d'événement encourage la pratique du sport. — *This kind of event encourages people to do sport.*
le festival d'Édimbourg — *the Edinburgh festival*
deux années de suite — *two years in a row*

Had a look ☐   Nearly there ☐   Nailed it ☐

M 8

---

*Take extra care with words that are very similar to words in English, for example:

l'ouragan	hurricane
le vent	wind
le gel	frost

**The *nous* form of the verb in the imperative tense is often used to convey the idea of doing something collectively.

Évitons la pollution! Let's avoid pollution!

ISBN 978-1-292-17256-9